English Code 2
Journey
Student's Book

Contents

Unit	Unit aims	Vocabulary	Language lab 1
1 Our world pp. 4–17	How can I create a nature scrapbook? • Use nature and direction words. • Give and understand instructions. • Describe where things are using *next to*, *behind*, *in front of*. • Understand and give instructions to play a game.	**Directions:** down, left, right, straight, up **Natural world:** bridge, rock, flower, forest, hill, path, tree	Language Lab 1 Walk. Don't walk.
2 Out and about! pp. 18–31	How can I create a town guide? • Use town words. • Talk about my town using *like* / *don't like*. • Describe places and things using *there is* / *there are*.	**Places:** café, castle, farm, house, library, museum, park, playground, river, school, store, swimming pool	Language Lab 1 I like parks. I don't like stores. Does she like playgrounds? He likes parks. She doesn't like stores.
Culture 1	Beautiful gardens	pp. 32–33	
3 Day and night pp. 34–47	How can I talk about day and night? • Use animal and daily routine words. • Talk about daily routines. • Ask and answer about daily routines.	**Animals:** bat, cow, donkey, goat, owl, porcupine **Daily Routine:** brush my teeth, eat, go to school, sleep, wake up, wash my face	Language Lab 1 I go to school. I don't go to school. Do you go to school? Yes, I do. / No, I don't.
4 At the gallery pp. 48–61	How can I create a portrait gallery? • Use describing words. • Describe people using *always* / *sometimes* / *never*. • Ask and answer about people and objects using *have*. • Talk about funny photos.	**Adjectives for People and Feelings:** angry, friendly, funny, happy, helpful, kind, lazy, naughty, sad, shy, tired, young	Language Lab 1 Is he sad? No, he isn't. He's happy.
Culture 2	Music around the world	pp. 62–63	
5 Come in! pp. 64–77	How can I create a class meal? • Use food words. • Ask for things politely using *Can I have …?* • Ask and answer about objects using *this* / *that*. • Ask and answer about food.	**Food and drink:** bread, cheese, chicken, cookies, fish, ice cream, juice, pasta, rice, salad, soup, water	Language Lab 1 Can I have some water, please? Sure! Can I ride your bike, please? Sorry, no!
6 Sports Day pp. 78–91	How can I organize a sports day? • Use sport and activity words. • Talk about actions using *I'm …ing*. • Ask and answer about actions using *Can you … ?* • Talk about activities with my friends.	**Sports:** basketball, catch, hit, jump, kick, run, soccer, table tennis, team, throw, volleyball, watch	Language Lab 1 I'm jumping. You're jumping. Are you swimming? Yes, I am. / No, I'm not.
Culture 3	Amazing boat races	pp. 92–93	

Values	Phonics	STEAM	Language lab 2	Project and Review
Show concern for each other.	s, sh, j, ch soup, sun, see shell, shoe, shop jeep, juice, jump cheese, cherry, chicken	Science: Landforms: mountains Experiment: Making mountains with towels	Language Lab 2 above, behind, in, in front of, near, next to, on, opposite, under	Make a nature scrapbook.
Listen to your friends.	a, e bag, cap, cat, man, mat, pan, clap leg, pen, peg, pet, ten, wet	Engineering: Building materials Experiment: Building a strong tower	Language Lab 2 There's a river. There are houses. There isn't a park. There aren't any farms.	Make a town guide.
Be prepared.	i, o bin, dig, hit, sing, sit, six dog, fox, hop, hot, jog, frog, stop	Science: Space systems: the Sun and Earth Experiment: Finding out how the earth and sun move	Language Lab 2 He eats three bananas. He doesn't eat apples. Does he eat bananas? Yes, he does. No, he doesn't.	Do a day and night presentation.
Ask people before you take photos.	j, y jacket, jaguar, jar, jeans, jog, juice, jump, jungle yak, yellow, yes, yo-yo, yogurt, you, young, yours	Art and design: Facial expressions: changing faces Experiment: Recording how we change and react to others' emotions and expressions	Language Lab 2 Do you have a brother? Yes, I do. He's funny! Do you have a sister? No, I don't.	Create a portrait gallery.
Be kind. Ask people what they like and don't like.	ch, sh chair, cheese, cherries, chess, chicken, chips sheep, shelf, ship, shirt, shoes, shop, shorts	Technology: Milk processes Experiment: Making ice cream	Language Lab 2 Can I have this salad, please? Can I have that salad, please?	Create a class meal. Pasta, chicken, and cheese Ice cream and mango Grapes and watermelon
I share my skills and help my friends to do things.	th that, there, these, they, this, those thank, things, thirteen, three, throw	Math: Measurement Experiment: Measuring the air in our lungs	Language Lab 2 Can you ride a bike? Yes, I can. No, I can't.	Organize a Sports Day.

4 Listen and point. Then sing along and dance.

SONG TIME

Climb up!

The **trees** are green.
The sky is blue.
I'm having fun in the trees
with you!

The trees are high.
The sky is, too.
I'm having fun in the trees
with you!

Climb **up**, climb up,
Climb up, climb very high!
Don't look **down**,
Look, look at the sky!

tree

climb up

look down

Are you up in a tree?
VOCABULARY

I will learn nature and direction words.

1 Listen, point, and repeat.

1 hill
2 bridge 
3 tree 
4 flower 
5 path 
6 forest 
7 rock 
8 left 
9 right 
10 up 
11 down 
12 straight 

2 Look and read. Put a check ✓ or cross ✗ in the box.

1 This is a hill. ☐
2 This is a tree. ☐
3 This is a path. ☐
4 This is a forest. ☐
5  This is a bridge. ☐

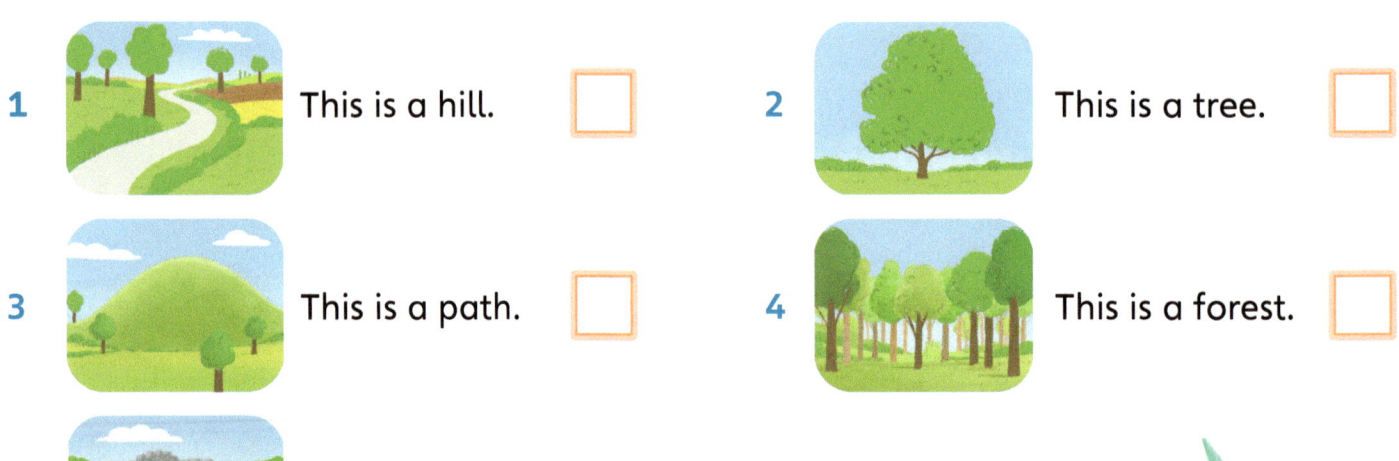

3 Label the picture. Use the words from 1.

4 Look at 3. Read. Then write the correct words.

1 The boy is walking **down** the hill. _____
2 The girl is climbing **up** the tree. _____
3 The dog **isn't** running straight. _____
4 The man is going **left**. _____
5 The woman is going **right**. _____
6 There are six **yellow** flowers. _____

5  Now listen, check, and say the sentences.

The boy is walking up the hill.

6 Make your own picture dictionary. Add any nature words you know.

flower   forest

seven 7

Language lab 1

GRAMMAR 1: WALK / DON'T WALK

I will understand and give instructions.

1 Watch. Then choose and write.

> Milly   Leo   Mrs. Hay's

1 Anna and _____ are going to _____ farm.

2 _____ has a brother and sister.

Walk   Don't walk.

2 Where is she going? Read and draw the correct path ↘.

1 Go straight.
2 Turn left.
3 Turn right.
4 Don't turn left. Turn right.
5 Go straight.
6 Don't turn right. Turn left.
7 Turn right. Stop.

The girl is going to the _____ .

3 Look at 2 again. Now complete the directions to the other place.

1 _____ straight. ↑
2 _____ right. →
3 _____ left. ←
4 _____ _____ right. _____ left. ←

5 _____ straight. ↑
6 _____ _____ _____ . Turn right. →
7 _____ left. _____ . ←

The girl is going to the _____ .

4 Listen and read. Then listen again and dance.

CODE CRACKER

Turn left!
Turn right!
Jump!
Stop!
Don't dance!

Turn left!
Turn right!
Jump!
Don't stop!
Jump, jump, jump!
Stop!

5 Create a dance for your friends. Use these words.

kick   jump   run   dance   stop   turn   walk

Don't stop!   Turn left!

Story lab
READING

I will read a story about helping others.

1  **Read and listen. Circle the new word.**

a forest   a bridge   a trampoline

2 Look at the story. Circle T (True) or F (False).

1. The children climb up.   T / F
2. Miss Kelly climbs on the bridge.   T / F
3. Mrs. Hay has lots of food.   T / F
4. Milly jumps down.   T / F
5. They all jump on the trampoline.   T / F

Values Show concern for each other.

3 Who is helping Milly? Read and check ✓ or cross ✗.

1. This is an amazing forest!
2. Get the trampoline!
3. I can see our school!

4 Act out the story in groups. How do you help your friends?

eleven 11

Phonics lab
S, SH, J, AND CH

I will learn the **s**, **sh**, **j**, and **ch** sounds.

1 **Listen and repeat. Then write s or sh.**

1 ____oup
2 ____un
3 ____oe
4 ____ell

2 **Listen and repeat. Then write j or ch.**

1 ____ump
2 ____uice
3 ____icken
4 ____erry

3 **Listen and chant.**

Chicken and cheese
and juice in the shop.
Soup in the shop,
Shells in the shop!

4 **Make shell shapes.**

Paint the shapes.

You can use pasta!
Put it on the refrigerator.

Stick a magnet.

5 **Listen and play the game.**

s = left   j = up
sh = right   ch = down

Experiment lab

SCIENCE: LANDFORMS

I will learn about landforms.

1 🎧 **Listen and read. Then label the picture.**

mountain   tectonic plate

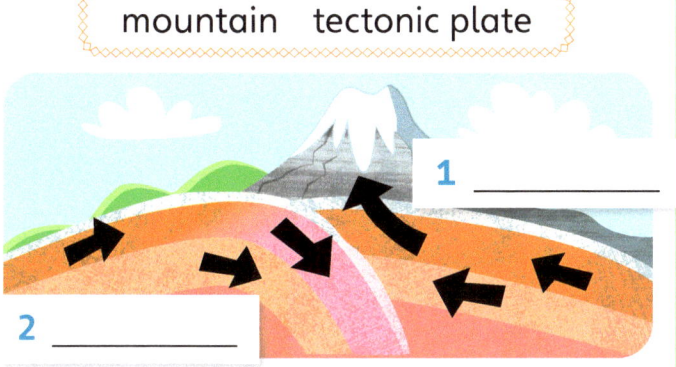

1 _____

2 _____

Land is made of rocks. There are many different rocks of different colors. Hills and mountains are made of rocks.

There are rocks under the earth. These rocks are called tectonic plates.

2 💡 **Count and write how many layers. Then ask and answer.**

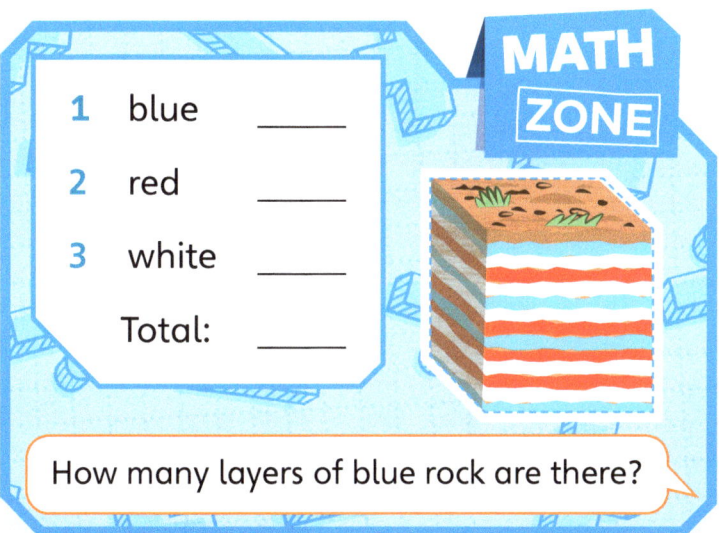

MATH ZONE

1 blue   _____
2 red   _____
3 white   _____
Total: _____

How many layers of blue rock are there?

EXPERIMENT TIME

How are mountains made?

1 Make mountains with towels.

Push!

Push quickly.
Push slowly.

2 Check ✓ or cross ✗.

1 I push and the towels …

   go up ☐

   go down ☐

   look like mountains ☐

2 I think …

   tectonic plates move ☐

   tectonic plates make mountains, hills, and volcanoes ☐

▶ **Watch a video about rocks.**

Language lab 2

GRAMMAR 2: ON, IN, UNDER, NEXT TO, BEHIND ...

I will use words to describe where things are.

1 Where are they? Read and check ☑ or cross ☒.

1. The gray and red bird is behind the tree.
2. The brown bird is in the tree.
3. The white bird is above the tree.
4. The black bird is opposite the tree.
5. The red and brown bird is near the tree.
6. The purple bird is near the tree.

2 Look. Then write.

in front of   under   on

1. The rabbit is _____ the tree.
2. The frog is _____ the flower.
3. The lizard is _____ the rock.

3 Look at 1 and 2. Ask and answer with a partner.

"Where's the blue bird?" "It's behind the tree."

14 fourteen

Draw a forest!
COMMUNICATION

I will understand and give instructions to play a game.

1 🎧 💡 **Listen and check ✓ the correct picture.**

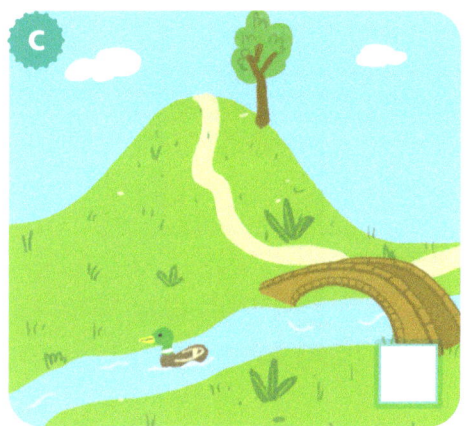

2 💬 **Play *Guess which picture*.**

Is the duck under the bridge?

Picture a!

No, it isn't.

3 🎧 🎨 **Now listen. Then draw.**

CODE CRACKER

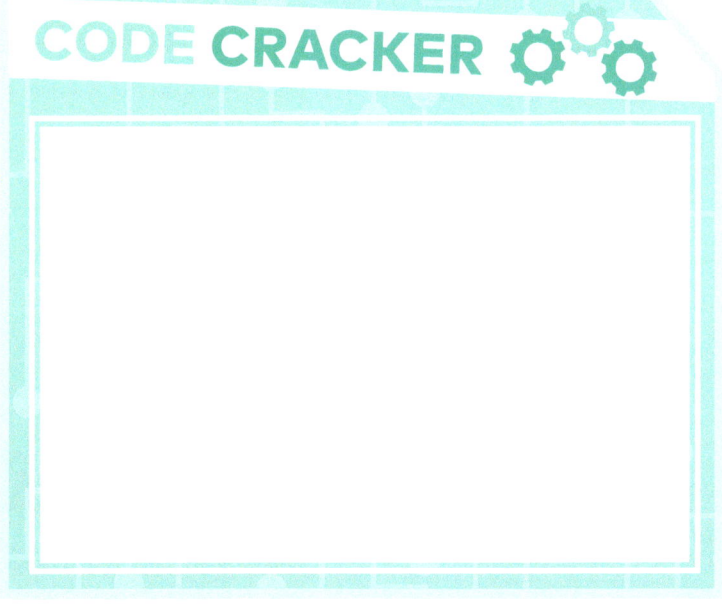

4 💬 **Choose and complete the sentences. Then tell your partner what to draw.**

Use these words.

> hill path forest tree
> bridge flower

1 Draw a _____

2 Draw a _____

3 The _____ is next to / in front of / under / on / behind / above / near the _____ .

fifteen 15

PROJECT AND REVIEW

Make a nature scrapbook

Step 1

Research

 What things from nature can you see in your town or country?

- ☐ Write down where they are or …
- ☐ … find out where they are.
- ☐ List things you see every day.
- ☐ Learn their names.

What's this flower?

It's a tulip.

Step 2

Plan

 How can I start my nature scrapbook?

- ☐ Decide what to put in your scrapbook.
- ☐ Choose how many pages you need for trees, birds, and flowers.
- ☐ Decide what photos you want and what things you will draw.

Write about …
- What it is
- Where it is
- Why I like it

Step 3

Create

> How can I create my nature scrapbook?

- [ ] Stick or draw pictures.
- [ ] Write about the pictures.
- [ ] Write where you can see natural things and why you like them.

Amazing rocks in Hunan, China.

Look out for flowers, birds, and trees when you travel to school. Count how many you see.

Step 4

Show and tell

> Share your work and ideas with friends.

"I like that idea!"
"Thank you."
"Where is that flower?"
"It's behind my house! I like the colors!"

Now I can ...

... use nature and direction words.

... give and understand instructions.

... describe where things are using **next to, behind, in front of.**

... understand and give instructions to play a game.

seventeen 17

3 Where can you find these things? Point and say.

CODE CRACKER

4 Listen and point. Then sing along and dance.

SONG TIME

Here, there, everywhere!

I like it here, I like it there,
I like it, like it everywhere!

There are **stores** and there's a **school**.
There's a **castle** and a **pool**!

I like it here, I like it there,
I like it, like it everywhere!

here!

there!

everywhere!

Where are they?

VOCABULARY

I will learn town words.

1 016 **Listen, point, and repeat.**

1 house

2 store

3 library

4 farm

5 museum

6 playground

7 park

8 café

9 river

10 swimming pool

11 castle

12 school

2 017 **Listen and circle.**

1 school / playground
2 café / castle
3 farm / museum
4 river / store

3 **Look at 1. Circle the places you like. Then say.**

I like the park!

I like the swimming pool and the farm!

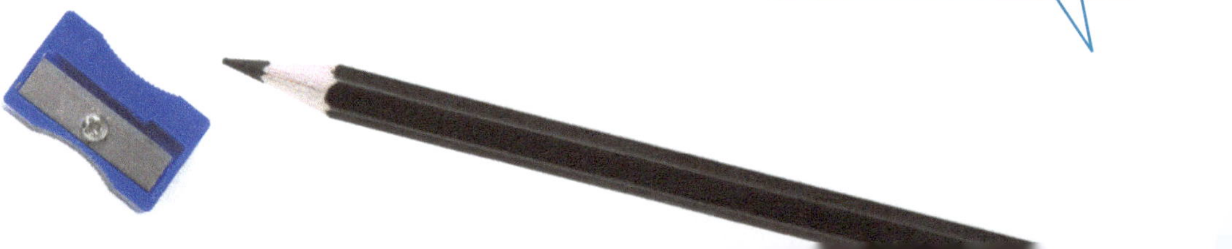

20 twenty

4 Mom is busy today! Read, draw, and number.

Go to the ...
1 park
2 library
3 farm
4 store
5 school

CODE CRACKER

5 Where are they? Write.

1 _farm_

2 _____

3 _____

4 _____

5 _____

6 _____

6 Where can you do these things? Write. Then say.

1 play _____
2 eat and drink _____
3 climb _____
4 swim _____

I can swim in a swimming pool.

I can eat and drink in a café.

7 Make your own picture dictionary. Draw and write town words.

castle   park

twenty-one 21

Language lab 1

GRAMMAR 1: LIKE / DON'T LIKE

*I will talk about town words using **like / don't like**.*

1  Watch. What does Milly like? Check ☑ or cross ☒.

I **like** parks. 😃
I **don't like** stores. ☹
Does she **like** playgrounds?
Yes, she does. / No, she doesn't.
He **likes** parks.
She **doesn't like** stores.

Milly likes …

2   Watch again and circle.

1 Anna **likes** / doesn't like clothes stores.
2 Milly **likes** / doesn't like cars.

3 Read and draw 😃 or ☹.

1 I don't like castles.
2 Leo doesn't like stores.
3 Milly likes farms.
4 I like museums.

4 Plan a day out with a partner. Ask and answer. Then write.

"Do you like parks?" "Yes, I do." "Do you like park a?" "No, I don't. I like park b."

1 I like park ___b___ .
2 I don't like _____ .
3 My partner likes _____ .
4 My partner doesn't like _____ .

"Do you like swimming pools?"

1 I _____ swimming pool _____ .
2 I don't _____ swimming pool _____ .
3 My partner _____ swimming pool _____ .
4 My partner doesn't _____ swimming pool _____ .

5 Which places do you like? Write for you and your partner. Now decide. Where do you want to go?

CODE CRACKER

	Me	My partner	Our choice
Park			
Pool			

6 Now talk about your choice.

"I like park a. Carla likes park c." "We both like swimming pool c!"

Values Listen to your friends.

7 How do you and your friends decide what to do? Check ✓ the correct box.

1 I only do what I want to do. ☐
2 I listen to my friends and we decide together. ☐

twenty-three 23

Story lab
READING

I will read a story about a town.

1 🔊 019 💬 **Read and listen. Why is it a special day in Castle Town?**

A special day

2. "Look! A band!"
"Wow! The town is beautiful today!"

1. "Listen, Anna! I can hear music!"
"What's happening, Leo?"
"I don't know!"

3. "I like the castle!"
"It's red and yellow!"

4. "Oh, no! Look, Anna!"
"Help! I can't stop!"

2 Look at the story. Then match and number.

 a
 b
 c
 d

1 Anna
2 Leo
3 Miss Kelly
4 Castle Town

24 twenty-four

3 Look at the story again. Then read and circle.

1 It plays music.   a band / the school
2 It's red and yellow.   the museum / the castle
3 It's 100 years old!   Castle Town / Miss Kelly

4 What makes the castle red and yellow today? Check ☑.

5 Act out the story in groups.

Phonics lab
A AND E

I will learn the a and e sounds.

1 Listen and repeat. Then write **a** or **e**.

1 c___p   2 b___g   3 m___t   4 p___g   5 t___n   6 p___t

2 Listen and chant.

A **man** and a **pan**.
Cats on a **mat**.
Ten **pets**.
Oh no! Oh no!
Ten wet **pets**!

3 Listen and play the game.

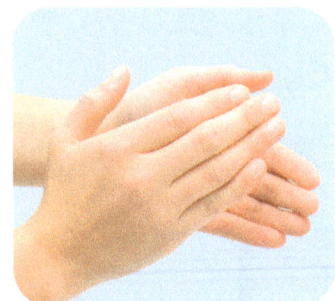 

a = clap   e = hop on one leg

4 Look and match.

Experiment lab
ENGINEERING: HOW TO BUILD A HOUSE

I will learn about building materials.

 Watch a video about buildings

1 What do we need to build a house? Check ✓ or cross ✗.

1 bricks

2 wood

3 cement

4 straws

5 steel

6 spaghetti

2 Now listen, read, and check your answers.

Houses are made of cement and bricks and steel. There is wood in this house, too. This house is strong.

3 Which house is strong? Look and circle a or b.

a

b

EXPERIMENT TIME

How can I build a tower?

Look! This is the Eiffel Tower.

1 Build a tower.

You need:
spaghetti
clay

You need:
cups
construction paper

2 Can you put books on your tower? Is it strong? Circle.

	Spaghetti tower	Cups tower
I can put books on my tower.	Yes / No	Yes / No
My tower is strong.	Yes / No	Yes / No

twenty-seven 27

Language lab 2

GRAMMAR 2: THERE IS / THERE ARE

I will describe places using there is / there are.

There is = There's

There's a river. 😃
There are houses. 😃
There isn't a playground. 🙁
There aren't any farms. 🙁

1 🎧 024 Listen and read.

We're at a miniature village. There are houses. There's a river. There are stores. There's a castle. There isn't a farm. There's a school. There aren't any museums. There are three cafés.

2 Now write about your town.

1 There _____ a school.
2 There _____ a castle.
3 There _____ houses.
4 There _____ museums.

3 Look, count, add, and write.

MATH ZONE

1 Houses in pictures a and b.
  _____ + _____ = _____
2 Stores in pictures a and b.
  _____ + _____ = _____

4 💬 Which picture is it? Ask and answer.

— Are there any houses?
— Yes! There are eleven houses.
— Picture a!

28 twenty-eight

Let's play!
COMMUNICATION

I will talk about games.

Let's make a castle.
Good idea!

1 Which game is it? Listen and write a, b, or c.

1 _____   2 _____   3 _____

a

b

c

2 Think about your favorite game. Talk about it with a partner using these words.

Let's play …   This is my favorite.
Me, too.   OK.   It's great.
There is/isn't/are/aren't …

Let's play with the farm.
OK!

3 Design a game. Draw and write.

My game is _____.
There's a/an _____.
There are _____.
There isn't/aren't any _____.

4 Now tell the class about your game.

Do you like my game? Look … there's a school, a river …

twenty-nine 29

PROJECT AND REVIEW

Make a town guide

Step 1

Research

 What's in my town?

- [ ] Think about your favorite places.
- [ ] Find photos.
- [ ] Find information and write notes.

What are my favorite places?

pool
library

Step 2

Plan

 What will you do?

- [ ] Plan a town guide.
- [ ] Read my notes.
- [ ] Choose places in my town.
- [ ] Draw or take photos of places in my town.

Step 3

Create

 How can I create my town guide?

- [ ] Design your page(s).
- [ ] Write about your town.
- [ ] Decorate your page(s).
- [ ] Check your work.

Step 4

Show and tell

 Present your guide.

- [ ] Talk to friends about your town.
- [ ] Are any places missing?

"Look, this is my house."

"And this is the castle."

+ Show a new friend around your town.

Now I can ...

... use town words.

... talk about my town using **like / don't like**.

... describe places and things using **there is / there are**.

Beautiful gardens
CULTURE 1

1 Look at the pictures. What places can you see? Say.

2 Listen and read.

The Lost Gardens of Heligan

Wow! It's a secret garden! It's very old!

Let's make it beautiful again!

The Lost Gardens of Heligan are very old. They are in Cornwall, England.

The gardens are beautiful now. There are giants in the gardens! The giants are made of rock.

This is a giant's head! Look at its hair. It's made of leaves and grass.

This giant is watching something!

This giant is tired. It's sleeping!

Singapore—the Garden City!

Fun Fact! You can grow plants on walls!

Singapore is a big city. There are lots of beautiful gardens. Many people live in apartments, and they don't have gardens or yards. But some people grow flowers on roofs and on walls. Plants, trees, and flowers make cities look beautiful, and they make oxygen.

3 Choose and complete.

walls   rocks   trees

1. There are giants made of _____ in the garden in Cornwall.
2. You can grow plants on _____ !
3. Plants, _____ , and flowers make our cities beautiful.

4 Talk to a partner about the gardens.

I like the garden on the roof!

Me, too! It looks fresh and green!

My Culture

Find out about interesting gardens in your country.

5 Design and make a garden in a pot.

1. Put earth in a flower pot.
2. Add stones and small flowers and plants.
3. You can have a castle, a house, a river, or a bridge in your garden.

6 Describe your garden in a pot.

This is my garden pot. It has purple flowers and a bridge!

3 Day and night
How can I talk about day and night?

1  Point and say **It's day/It's night**.

2 When do they wake up? Stick the animals on the picture.

3 Who am I? Check ✓ or cross ✗.

CODE CRACKER

1. I'm brown.
2. ... and I have four legs.
3. ... and I play at night.
4. I'm a/an

4 Listen and point. Then sing along and dance.

SONG TIME — Wonderful things

In the day, in the day, I **wake up**,
And la, la, la, I sing!
At night, at night, I **sleep**,
And dream of wonderful things.

La, la, la, I sing
La, la, la, I sing
La, la, la, I sing
I dream of wonderful things!

At night, at night, the owl wakes up,
And twit, twit, twoo, he sings!
In the day, in the day, he sleeps
And dreams of wonderful things.

wake up!
sing!
twit twoo
sleep!

What is it?

VOCABULARY

I will learn animal and daily routine words.

1 Listen, point, and repeat.

1 cow

2 goat

3 donkey

4 owl

5 porcupine

6 bat

7 eat

8 wake up

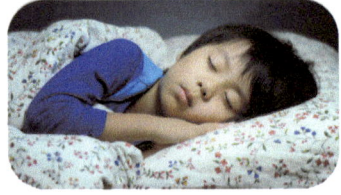
9 sleep

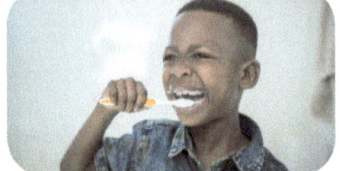
10 brush my teeth

11 wash my face

12 go to school

2 Label the pictures. Use the words and phrases in 1.

a

b

1 ___bat___   2 _____   1 ___sleep___   2 _____
3 _____   4 _____   3 _____   4 _____

Values Be prepared.

3 When do you need these things? Circle.

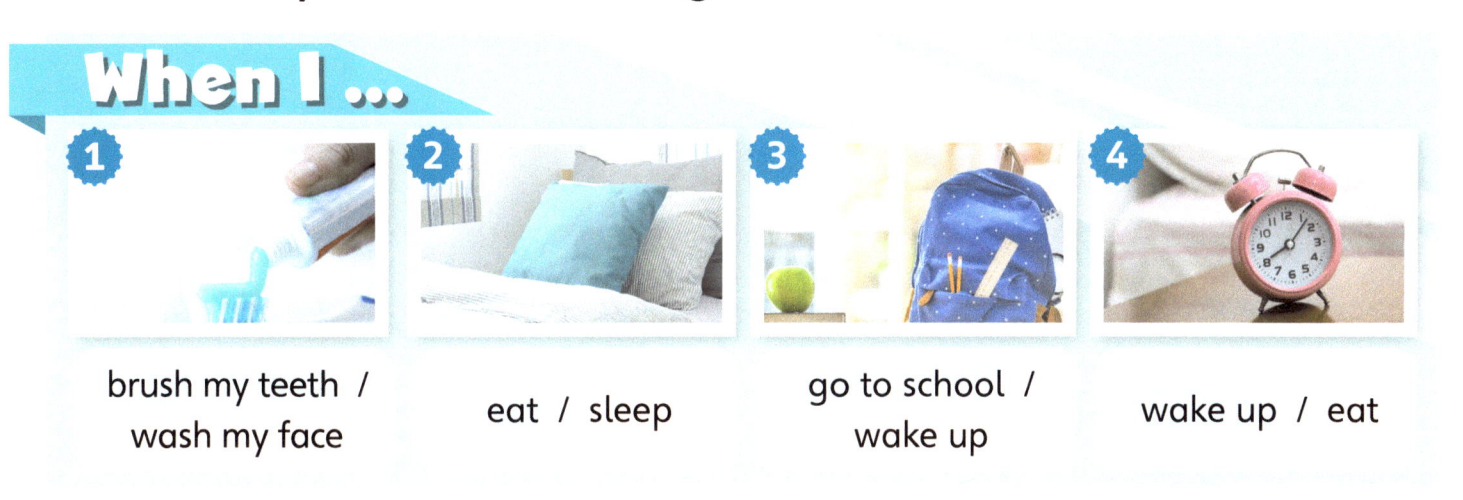

When I ...

1. brush my teeth / wash my face

2. eat / sleep

3. go to school / wake up

4. wake up / eat

4 Check ✓ or cross ✗.

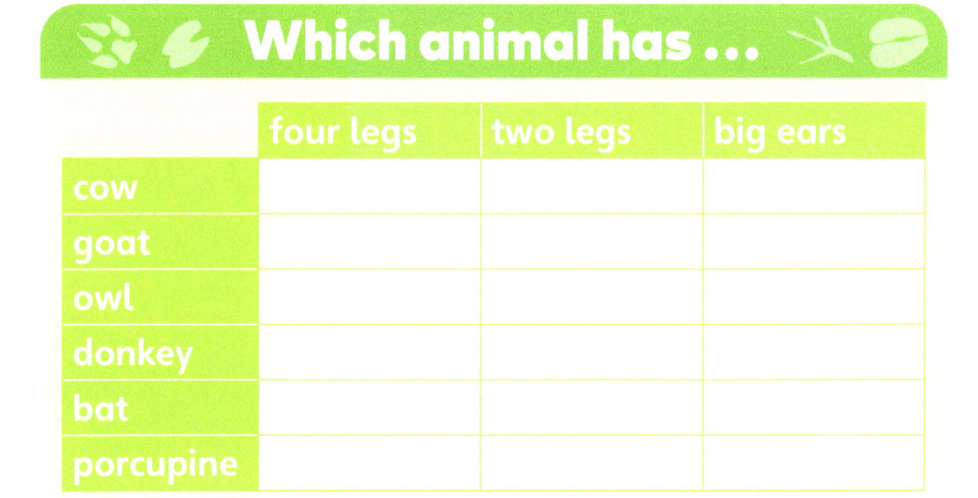

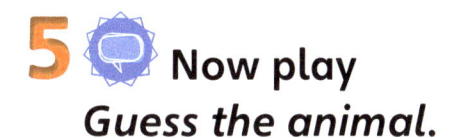

Which animal has ...

	four legs	two legs	big ears
cow			
goat			
owl			
donkey			
bat			
porcupine			

5 Now play *Guess the animal*.

It has four legs and big ears.

A donkey!

6 Make your own picture dictionary. Draw and write animal and daily routine words.

owl

porcupine

thirty-seven

Language lab 1

GRAMMAR 1: I GO / DON'T GO

I will talk about daily routines.

1 Watch. What is Leo talking about? Check ✓ the correct picture.

1. 2. 3. 4.

2 What do *you* think owls say? Write the sound.

Owls say _____

3 What do you and your friends do at school? Check ✓ or cross ✗. Then write We … /We don't … .

☐ eat ☐ sleep
☐ play ☐ sing
☐ brush our teeth ☐ read

At school …

1 We _____
2 _____
3 _____
4 _____
5 _____
6 _____

😀 **I go** to school.
   We go to school.
☹️ **I don't go** to school.
   We don't go to school.
❓ **Do you go to** school?
   Yes, I do. / No, I don't.

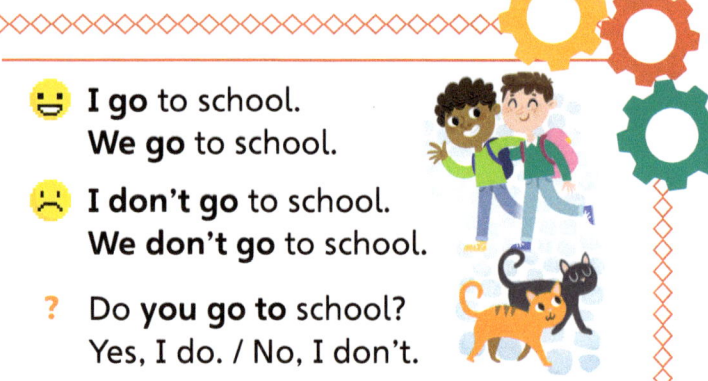

4 Choose and complete the questions. Circle *Yes* or *No*. Then listen and check.

brush   wash   eat   sleep   wake   swim

Quiz Time!

1 Do cats _____ their faces?

   Yes   No

   Do you _____ your face?

   _____

2 Do porcupines _____ in rivers?

   Yes   No

   Do you _____ in rivers?

   _____

3 Do bats _____ at night?

   Yes   No

   Do you _____ at night?

   _____

4 Do cows _____ their teeth?

   Yes   No

   Do you _____ your teeth?

   _____

5 Do goats _____ grass?

   Yes   No

   Do you _____ grass?

   _____

6 Do donkeys _____ up in the morning?

   Yes   No

   Do you _____ in the morning?

   _____

5 Look at **4** again and write answers for you.

6 Play *True or False* with a partner.

Goats don't eat grass.   False!

I brush my teeth.   True!

thirty-nine   39

Story lab
READING

I will read a story about farm animals.

1 🎧 031 **Read and listen. What farm animals can you see?**

Do goats dance?

1 Look, girls and boys. This is a cow. It eats grass.

2 Do cows sing, Miss Kelly?

No, Tom! They don't sing. They say "moo!"

3 This is a goat. Goats eat grass and fruit.

4 Do goats dance, Miss Kelly?

No, Tom! They don't dance!

2 💡 **Look at the story. Read and circle T (True) or F (False).**

1. Miss Kelly is a teacher. T / F
2. They go to Mrs. Hay's farm. T / F
3. The cow doesn't like the song. T / F
4. Mrs. Hay's animals dance and sing. T / F

3 💡 💬 **Match. Then say who is speaking.**

1. On the •   • a happening?
2. What's •   • b bus!
3. I don't •   • c girls and boys.
4. Look, •   • d know!

What's happening?

Miss Kelly is speaking.

40 forty

5
On the bus!
To Mrs. Hay's farm, please!

6
Hello, Mrs. Hay. What's happening?
I don't know!

7
They like the music! They like this song!

8
Miss Kelly ... cows sing and goats dance!
Yes, Tom!

4 **Where do the animals go? Look at the animal footprints and write go or don't go.**

1. The cats _____ to the house.
2. The cats _____ to the park.
3. The donkeys _____ to the house.
4. The donkeys _____ to the park.

5 **Act out the story in groups.**

forty-one 41

Phonics lab
I AND O

I will learn the i and o sounds.

1 🎧 032 **Listen and repeat. Then write i or o.**

1 d___g   2 b___n   3 h___t

4 f___x   5 j___g   6 h___t

2 🎧 033 💬 **Listen and chant.**

Sit and sing,
Sit and sing,
Six little children sit and sing!

Jog, jog, jog!
Hop, hop, hop!
Stop!
The dog and the frog are hot, hot, hot!

3 🎧 034 💬 **Listen and play the game. Jump to i or o!**

4 Trace and match.

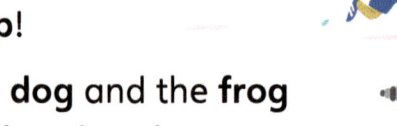

i   o

42 forty-two

Experiment lab

SCIENCE: THE SUN AND THE EARTH

I will learn about the Earth and the Sun.

1. Listen and read. Look at the pictures and write 1–4.

1. We see the Sun in the sky. It's day.
2. The Sun shines on the Earth.
3. The Earth goes round and round in 24 hours. That is a day.
4. The Earth goes around the Sun in 12 months. That is a year.

a — It's night. It's day.
b
c
d

2. Circle T (True) or F (False).

1. We see the Earth in the sky. T / F
2. There are 24 hours in a day. T / F
3. There are 12 months in a year. T / F

12 hours day + 12 hours night = 24 hours. We say "a day."

EXPERIMENT TIME

How does the Earth move?

1 Make an Earth and a Sun.

Make a green and blue ball. That is the Earth.

Make a big yellow circle. That is the Sun.

2 Check ✓ and say.

Look! The Earth goes around the Sun. ☐

Look! The Sun goes around the Earth. ☐

3 Move your Earth around the Sun with a partner and say the sentence in 2 again.

▶ Watch a video about space.

forty-three 43

Language lab 2

GRAMMAR 2: SHE EATS / DOESN'T EAT

I will ask and answer about daily routines.

1 What's wrong? Correct the sentences. Then listen and check.

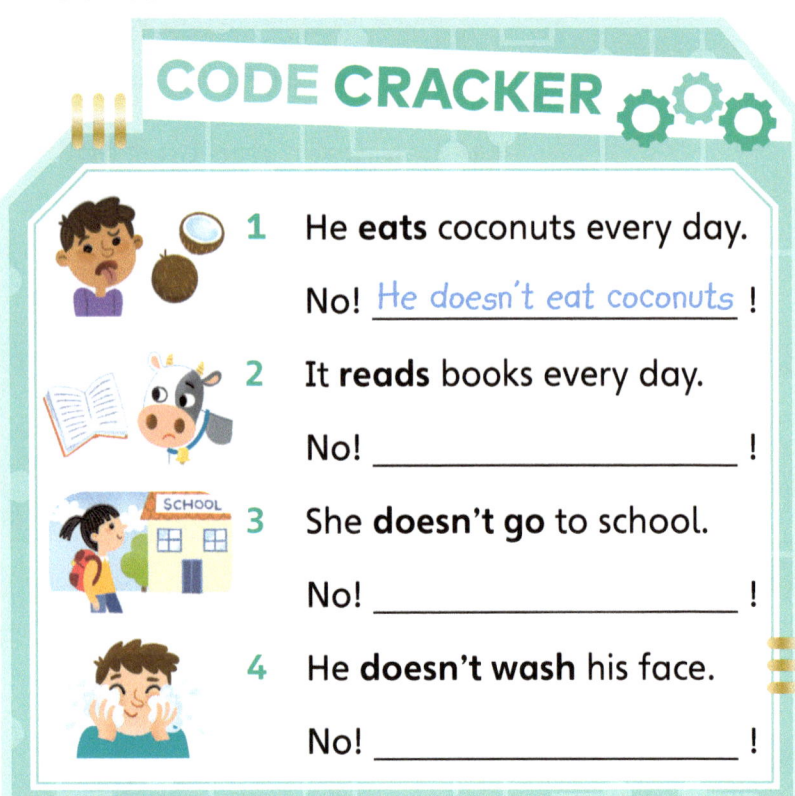

CODE CRACKER

1 He **eats** coconuts every day.
   No! *He doesn't eat coconuts* !

2 It **reads** books every day.
   No! _____ !

3 She **doesn't go** to school.
   No! _____ !

4 He **doesn't wash** his face.
   No! _____ !

He eats three bananas every day!
He doesn't eat apples.
Does he eat bananas?
Yes, **he does**.
No, **he doesn't**.

2 Choose. Then ask and answer with a partner.

read   eat an apple
go to the museum

Do you eat an apple every day?
No, I don't.

3 Write Yes, he does/No, he doesn't/Yes, she does/No, she doesn't.

1 Does your partner read every day?   _____
2 Does your partner eat an apple every day?   _____
3 Does your partner go to the museum every day?   _____

4 Now tell the class about your partner.

Bella reads every day.

What time is it?
COMMUNICATION

I will ask and answer about time and daily routines.

1 Write the missing numbers on the clock.

eight   two   three   twelve   six   ten

MATH ZONE

eleven ___ ___ one
___
nine ___
___
___ four
seven ___ ___ five
___

2 What time do you do these things? Write the number below.

a ____ o'clock
b ____ o'clock
c ____ o'clock
d ____ o'clock
e ____ o'clock
f ____ o'clock

3 Ask and answer with a partner. Then tell the class.

Do you wake up at seven o'clock?

No, I don't. I wake up at six o'clock.

Does Katy wake up at seven o'clock?

No, she doesn't. She wakes up at six o'clock.

4 Play the game.

What time is it?

It's three o'clock!

forty-five 45

PROJECT AND REVIEW

Do a day and night presentation

Step 1

Research

> How are day and night different?

- [ ] Write down a list of things that you see in the day.
- [ ] Write down a list of things that you see at night.
- [ ] Find out which animals sleep in the day and which sleep at night.
- [ ] Research why some animals sleep in the day and some at night.

Cows and goats sleep at night.

It's night. We can see the moon.

It's day. We can see the sun.

Step 2

Plan

> How can I plan my presentation?

- [ ] In teams, choose two things that are different in the day and at night.
- [ ] Choose one animal you want to talk about. Does it sleep in the day or at night? Why?
- [ ] Practice what to say.

Step 3

Create

> How can I create props?

- [ ] Make an animal mask.
- [ ] Make a sun and moon.
- [ ] Label your work.
- [ ] Make a poster for your presentation.

Choose an animal. Find out more. Tell your friends.

"Porcupines have big teeth! They eat wood!"

Step 4

Show and tell

> Share your day and night presentation with friends.

- [ ] Do a day and night presentation.
- [ ] Do animal movements.
- [ ] Talk about animals.

"I'm an owl!"

"I don't sleep at night! Twit twoo!"

Now I can ...

... use animal and daily routine words.

... talk about daily routines.

... ask and answer about daily routines.

forty-seven 47

4 At the gallery

How can I create a portrait gallery?

1 Which painting do you like? Point and say.

2 Stick the frames on the happy, sad, and angry paintings.

3 Order the pictures. Write 1–4.

CODE CRACKER

A   B
C   D

4 Listen and point. Then sing along and dance.

SONG TIME

My friends

He's never **angry**,
He's sometimes **shy**.
He's always **kind** and **happy**.
He's my friend, he's my friend!

She's never angry.
She's sometimes shy.
She's always kind and happy.
She's my friend, she's my friend!

angry!
shy!
happy!

forty-nine 49

I am happy!

VOCABULARY

I will learn describing words for people and pets.

1 🎧 💬 Listen, point, and repeat.

1 angry
2 happy
3 sad
4 funny
5 kind
6 friendly
7 shy
8 helpful
9 naughty
10 lazy
11 young
12 tired

2 💡 Who am I? Read 3 clues. Then circle a or b.

1. I'm happy.
   I'm helpful.
   I'm not old.

   a   b

2. I'm sad.
   I'm lazy.
   I'm not funny.

   a   b

3. I'm funny.
   I'm friendly.
   I'm not young.

   a   b

4. I'm shy.
   I'm young.
   I'm not angry.

   a   b

3 Now say three clues about the pictures for your partner to guess.

CODE CRACKER

I'm happy. I'm helpful. I'm old.

1 b!

4 Label the people and pets. Use all the words from **1**.

1 _____	2 _____	3 _____	4 _____
5 _____	6 _____	7 _____	8 _____
9 _____	10 _____	11 _____	12 _____

5 Now point at **4** and say.

I like this man. He is funny!

6 Make headbands and play the *Mime* game.

Am I shy?
I'm Sad
Am I sad?
No, you aren't.
Yes, you are!

7 Make your own picture dictionary. Draw happy, sad, and funny faces and write.

happy

sad

fifty-one 51

Language lab 1

GRAMMAR 1: HE / SHE   IS / ISN'T

*I will describe people using **always / sometimes / never**.*

1 Watch. Circle the correct word.

Leo is   sad / shy / angry .

Is he sad?
No, **he isn't**.
He's happy.

2 What do you think? Look, choose, and write.

She/He is …   She/He isn't …   Yes, she/he is.   No, she/he isn't.

1

Is she happy? _____

_____

_____ friendly.

_____ sad.

2

Is he tired? _____

_____ young.

_____ angry.

3

Is she shy? _____

_____ old.

_____ friendly.

3 Talk about your ideas. Work with a partner.

Look at Picture 1 … she's happy.

Is she happy, or is she sad?

He is **always** happy.   She is **sometimes** happy.   He is **never** happy.

4 Listen and circle.

friendly: always / sometimes / never   naughty: always / sometimes / never

5 Ask your partner. Then check ✓ or cross ✗.

	always	sometimes	never
friendly			
naughty			
helpful			
lazy			
shy			
happy			

Are you lazy?

No, I'm never lazy.

Oh, I'm sometimes lazy!

6 Look at 5. Write your partner's answers.

He's/She's   always/sometimes/never

1 _____ lazy.
2 _____ naughty.
3 _____ helpful.
4 _____ friendly.
5 _____ shy.
6 _____ happy.

7 Play *Who is it?* in groups.

She's sometimes shy. She's never lazy.

Is it Amy?

Yes, it is!

fifty-three 53

Story lab
READING

I will read a story about a painting competition.

1 🔊 💬 **Read and listen. Who wins the gold cup?**

Who is this?

1
- I have my paints.
- Great! I have pencils and crayons.
- I have a photo!

2 Who is this, Tom?
- It's my cousin. He's sometimes naughty and always happy!

3 Who is this, Mrs. Hay?
- It's my friend.
- Is she angry? She looks angry.
- Er … no … she's sad.

4 This is very good, Mr. Mud!
- Thank you. Milly is sometimes naughty, but she is friendly.

2 **Look at the story. Then read, choose, and write.**

rainbow   friend   cousin   Milly

1 Tom paints his _____ .

2 Mrs. Hay paints her _____ .

3 Mr. Mud paints _____ .

4 Milly paints a _____ .

54 fifty-four

5 OK, finish your pictures now, please!

6 The gold cup goes to … Mr. Mud!
Congratulations, Mr. Mud!

7 Look at Milly!

8 It's a rainbow! Milly, you are very funny!

3 Look at the story again. What are they like? Match and say.

1.
2.
3.

a She's sad.

b She's sometimes naughty, but she is friendly.

c He's sometimes naughty and always happy.

Is Tom's cousin sad?
No, he isn't. He's always happy!

4 Look at the story again. Then number the sentences in order.

a The gold cup goes to … Mr. Mud!

b Who is this, Mrs. Hays?

c Look at Milly!

d Is she angry? She looks angry.

e It's a rainbow! Milly, you are very funny!

5 Act out the story in groups.

fifty-five 55

Phonics lab
J AND Y

I will learn the j and y sounds.

1 **Listen and repeat. Then write j or y.**

1 ___eans
2 ___uice
3 ___ar
4 ___oung
5 ___ogurt
6 ___ak

2 **Listen and chant.**

Is it **your yellow yo-yo**, is it **yours**?
Is it **your yellow yo-yo**, is it **yours**?
Yes, yes, yes!

Jump in the **jungle**,
Jump, jump, jump!
Jump like a **jaguar**,
Jump, jump, jump!

3 **Listen and play the game.**

J = arms up   Y = arms crossed

4 **Make invisible words. Write with lemon juice.**

Experiment lab
ART AND DESIGN: CHANGING FACES

I will learn about changing faces.

▶ Watch a video about faces.

1 🎧 045 **Listen and read. Then circle.**

We have **muscles** in our faces. The muscles move our mouths, eyes, noses, and eyebrows.

muscles

Sometimes our eyes look big, and sometimes they look small. Sometimes our mouths look small, and sometimes they are big and open.

Artists paint and draw the muscles in a face. They use colors and lines and different shapes.

1    2    I can see muscles in picture 1 / 2 .

2 Match. There is one extra sentence.

He looks angry.   He is tired.

He looks sad.   He is happy.

EXPERIMENT TIME

How do you change?

1 💬 Work with a partner. One person laughs, yawns, or cries. What happens to you?

My partner	Me
laughs 	I laugh . / I don't laugh .
yawns 	I yawn . / I don't yawn .
cries 	I cry . / I don't cry .

2 Now circle for you.

I always / sometimes / never do the same as my partner.

fifty-seven 57

Language lab 2

GRAMMAR 2: DO YOU HAVE …?

I will ask and answer about people and objects using have.

1 Complete the questions. Then answer Yes, I do or No, I don't.

have
you
Do

Do you have a brother?
Yes, I do. He's funny!

Do you have a sister?
No, I don't.

1 _____ you have a cousin? _____

2 Do you _____ a bird? _____

3 Do _____ have a red hat? _____

4 _____ _____ _____ a blue pencil case? _____

2 Play *Tic Tac Toe* with a partner.

Yes, I do = ✓   No, I don't = ✗

cat	rabbit	red bag
green eraser	brother	silver ruler
white teddy	blue coat	sister

Do you have a red bag?

No, I don't.

It's a rabbit.
Its fur is white.

3 🎧 046 Listen and read. Then circle and write.

It's   Its

Do you have a cat?

Yes, I do. It's orange. Its fur is soft.

1 Do you have a dog?
   Yes, I do. _____
   black / white .
   _____ tail is
   brown / black .

2 Do you have a rabbit?
   Yes, I do. _____
   white / gray .
   _____ nose is
   blue / pink .

58 fifty-eight

Let's take a photo!
COMMUNICATION

I will talk about funny photos.

1 Listen and read.

1. This is my new phone. Its camera is really good.
   Let's take a photo.
   Yes, a selfie!
2. Okay … now … wait.
3. Oh, that's a funny photo!

2 Choose a funny photo. Work with a partner. Ask and answer.

Do you have orange hair? — No, I don't.
Are you sad? — Yes, I am.
Number 1!

Values Ask people before you take photos.

3 Who wants a photo? Check ✓ or cross ✗. Then listen and check.

Let's take a photo.

4 Read. Then circle for you.

I take photos of my friends.
I ask / don't ask my friends.

PROJECT AND REVIEW

Create a portrait gallery

Step 1

Research

▷ Who shall I paint?

☐ Think about what questions to ask them.

☐ Collect some paintings and photos for ideas.

Who to paint?

My friend?   Mom?

My cousin?   Me?

Our teacher?

Step 2

Plan

▷ What do we need to do and ask?

☐ Interview the people we are painting.

☐ Get paints, paper, glue, pencils, and crayons.

☐ Choose a style of painting.

☐ Decide where to display the pictures.

● What's your name?
● Are you always happy?
● Do you have a pet?
● What's your favorite color?

60 sixty

Step 3

Create

> How do we create our portrait gallery?

- [ ] Draw, paint, or take photos.
- [ ] Write about the people.
- [ ] Put the work on a wall.

Talk about old and new photos.

Look!

Step 4

Show and tell

> Talk about the people and the paintings.

Who's this?

It's our teacher! She's always kind.

She looks happy! It's a great painting!

Here, she looks funny and friendly.

Now I can ...

- ... use describing words.
- ... describe people using **always** / **sometimes** / **never**.
- ... ask and answer about people and objects using **have**.
- ... talk about funny photos.

sixty-one 61

Music around the world
CULTURE 2

1 Look at the pictures. What instruments can you see? Say.

2 Listen and read.

Drums

sticks

You bang drums.

These girls and boys are from Japan. They play drums. Their drums are round and hard. They are made from wood. The drums are heavy!

Bagpipes

pipes

bag

You blow bagpipes.

This boy is from Scotland. He plays the bagpipes. He is called a piper.
Bagpipes have a soft bag and long pipes.

Fun Fact!
Some drums are as big as cars!

Veenas

strings

neck

You play the strings on veenas.

This woman is from India. She plays a veena. Veenas are big and round. They have a long neck. They have strings. Very good music comes from light veenas, not heavy veenas.

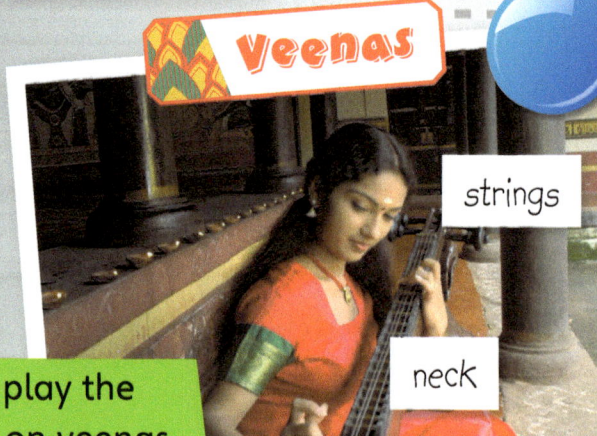

3 🎧 050 **What is it? Listen to the music and check ☑.**

It's a …	veena	bagpipe	drum
1			
2			
3			

4 🎧 051 **Listen again. How does the music make you feel? Choose and write.**

> happy   sad   angry   tired   good   bad   lazy

1 I feel _____ .   2 I feel _____ .   3 I feel _____ .

5 💬 **Now tell a partner.**   *It's happy music! I feel good!*

My Culture

Find out about traditional instruments in your country.

6 🔧 **Make a string instrument.**

1 Take a tissue box. Fold and stick card on the box.
2 Stick pins in the box.
3 Put the rubber bands around the pins.
4 Play your instrument!

It has strings. It's not heavy.

7 💬 **Describe your instrument.**

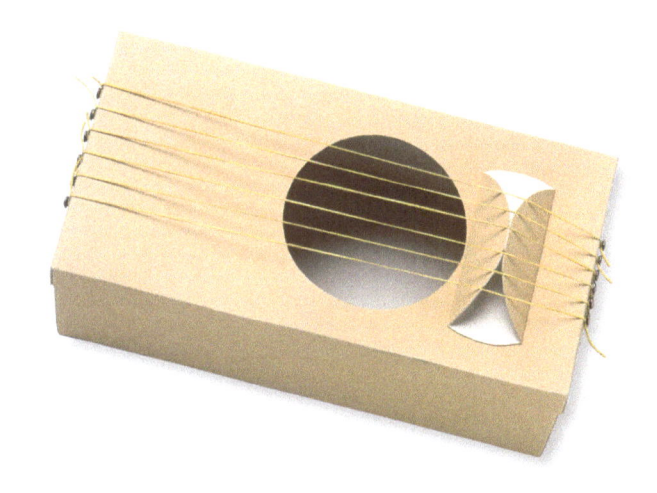

sixty-three 63

5 Come in!

How can I create a class meal?

1 What do you like in this house? Point and say.

2 Stick the food on the table. Then draw lines to match.

64 sixty-four

3 What do you say? Circle.

CODE CRACKER

1. Thank you! / Come in! 
2. Thank you! / Hello! 
3. Goodbye! / Come in!

4 Listen and point. Then sing along and dance.

Come in!

SONG TIME

Make yourself at home!

Come in and make yourself at home,
We're happy that you're here,
Come in and make yourself at home,
It's great to have you here.

Would you like some **pasta**?
Would you like some **cheese**?
Would you like some **cookies**?

Yes, please!

Repeat chorus

Would you like …?

sixty-five 65

Do you like cookies?
VOCABULARY

I will learn food words.

1 Listen, point, and repeat.

1 chicken
2 cheese
3 bread
4 rice
5 soup
6 salad
7 cookies
8 water
9 juice
10 ice cream
11 pasta
12 fish

2 You have $20. What would you like in the café? Decide and write.

MATH ZONE

ICE CREAM $4
$3
$3
$6
$7
$8
$1
$5
$4

How much is it?

_____ $_____
_____ $_____
_____ $_____
_____ $_____
_____ $_____

TOTAL $_____

How much do you have left? $_____

3 Look, match, and write the food.

1 — a Café menu

2 — b Grocery list

3 — c Make a sandwich!

4 Look at 3. Then ask and answer.

- She has fish and soup.
- 3 a !
- Yes!
- Do you like fish?
- Yes, I do. I don't like soup!

5 Now ask and answer with a partner.

- I have soup.
- How much is it?
- It's six dollars. And you?
- I have cookies and water.

6 Make your own picture dictionary. Draw or write your favorite food words.

ice cream   salad

sixty-seven 67

Language lab 1

GRAMMAR 1: CAN I HAVE ...?

I will ask for things politely using **Can I have ...?**

1 Watch. What does Leo ask for? Check ✓ or cross ✗.

fish ☐   rice ☐   bread ☐   apples ☐
oranges ☐   chicken ☐   pasta ☐   bananas ☐

2 Watch again. Then choose and write.

Milly   Leo and his friends
Mrs. Hay

The food is for _____ .

Can I have some water, please? — Sure!

Can I ride your bike, please? — Sorry, no!

3 What do they need? Look, choose, and write.

bread   pasta   cheese   rice

1 Can I have some _____ , please?
2 Can I have _____ , please?
3 Can I _____ ?
4 _____

68   sixty-eight

4 Order and write to find out what they need. Then match a–e.

CODE CRACKER

pencil   a   have   I

1 Can _____ , please? ☐

I   please   water   some   have   Can

2 _____ , _____ ? ☐

have   I   Can   a   please   bag

3 _____ , _____ ? ☐

an   Can   please   I   have   eraser

4 _____ , _____ ? ☐

some   have   please   can   cookies   we

5 _____ , _____ ? ☐

5 Play the game. Ask and answer.

Can I have two apples, please?

Sorry, no!

Can I have one apple?

Sure!

Story lab
READING

I will read a story about Tom's cousin.

1 🎧 💬 **Read and listen. Who comes to Tom's house?**

Come over and play!

1. It's nine o'clock! School! I'm late!
   Tom, it's Saturday. No school today!
   Hooray!

2. Can I play with my toys, Mom?
   Yes, sure!

3. Tom, look! Grandma and Aunt Julia are here! And your cousin, Adam!
   Come in!
   Hello, Tom!

4. Can I have some water, please?
   Can I have some juice, please?
   Yes, of course!

2 Circle T (True) or F (False).

1. This is my grandma.  T / F
2. This is my aunt.  T / F
3. This is my mom.  T / F
4. This is my cousin.  T / F

3 Complete and match.

1. Can I _____ with my toys, Mom?
2. Can I have _____ water, please?
3. Can I _____ this book?

- a Okay.
- b Yes, sure!
- c Yes, of course!

70 seventy

5 Can I have this car? Er ... okay.

6 Oh dear! I'm sorry, Tom! Can I have this book? Er ... okay.

7 Sorry, Tom! I have a good idea! Let's make a cake! Yes! Good idea!

8 This is fun! Yes, it is!

4 Look and think. What toys does Adam play with? Check ✓ or cross ✗.

a b c d e f

5 Act out the story in groups.

Phonics lab
CH AND SH

I will learn the ch and sh sounds.

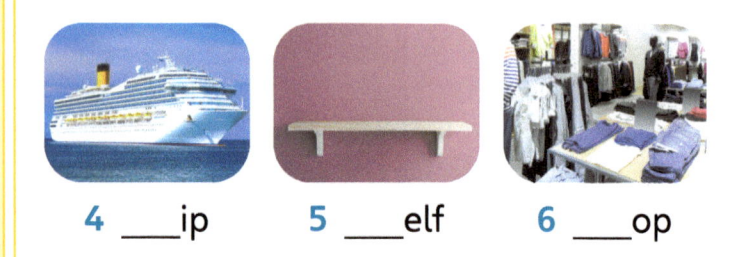

1 Listen and repeat. Then write **ch** or **sh**.

1 ___air   2 ___ips   3 ___ess

4 ___ip   5 ___elf   6 ___op

2 Listen and chant.

Chicken and cherries, chips and cheese!
Yes, please!
Chicken and cherries, chips and cheese!

A shirt in the shop.
Shoes in the shop.
Shorts in the shop.
And a sheep in the shop!

3 Listen and play the game.

ch = dance   sh = stop!

4 Make shapes and play with a partner.

Sh sh sh
Yes!
Is it a shirt?
sheep
sh

72 seventy-two

Experiment lab

TECHNOLOGY: MILK

I will learn about making milk.

▶ Watch a video about milk.

1 🎧 059 **Listen, read, and match. Write a–d.**

| a | b |
| c | d |

We get milk from animals: cows, sheep, goats, and horses 1 ☐. We also get milk from plants like coconuts, almonds, and soya beans 2 ☐.

Farmers pick the nuts and beans from trees and plants. They sometimes use combine harvesters to help them 3 ☐. The nuts and beans go to factories 4 ☐. Machines get the milk from the plants and make it clean and healthy.

2 💬 **Talk with a partner.**

Do you drink milk from goats?

Yes, I do!

EXPERIMENT TIME

Can you make ice cream?

You can use plant or animal milk!

1 Milk, sugar, and vanilla

2 Ice and salt

The salt makes the ice extra cold!

5 minutes!

3 Close the bags!

4 Shake, shake, shake!

Open the small bag.
Do you have ice cream?
Yes / No

seventy-three 73

Language lab 2

GRAMMAR 2: CAN I HAVE THIS / THAT ...?

*I will ask and answer about objects using **this / that**.*

1 Choose and complete. Write **this** or **that** ...

1   Can I have _____ _____ , please?
2   Can I have _____ _____ , please?
3   Can I have _____ _____ , please?

2 Read and check ☑.

1   a   b
    Can I have an ice cream, please?
    This one or that one?
    That one!

2   a   b
    Can I have a salad, please?
    This one or that one?
    This one!

3   a   b
    Can I have a juice, please?
    This one or that one?
    This one!

Can I have this salad, please?

Can I have that salad, please?

3 Play *This or That*.

Can I have a book, please?

Sure! This one or that one?

This one! No ... that one!

74 seventy-four

Let's order some food!
COMMUNICATION

I will ask and answer about food.

1 Complete the conversations. Then read them with a partner.

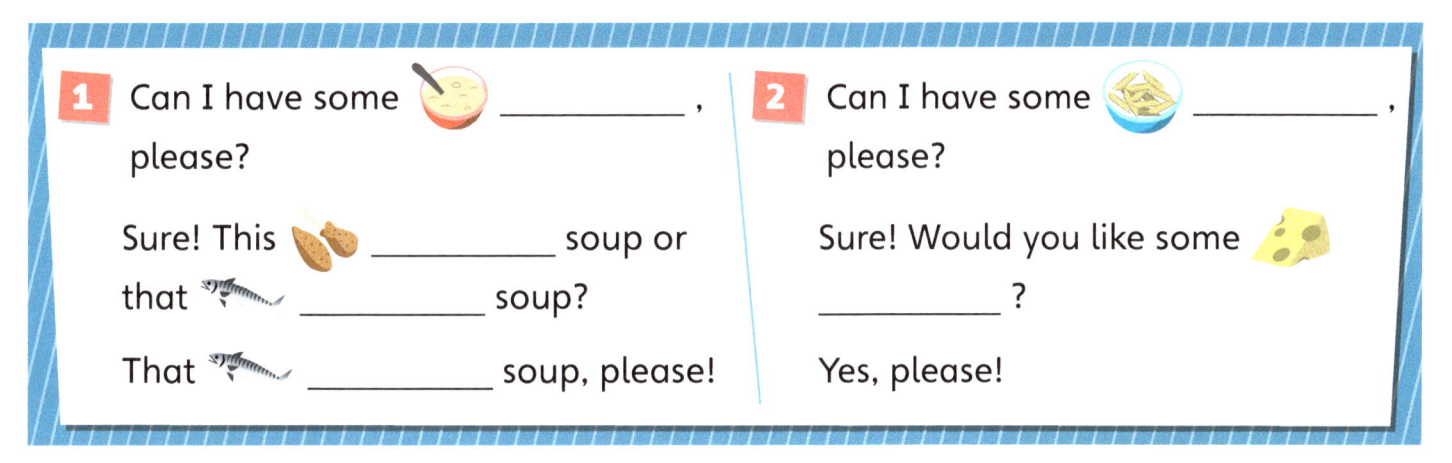

1. Can I have some _____, please?
   Sure! This _____ soup or that _____ soup?
   That _____ soup, please!

2. Can I have some _____, please?
   Sure! Would you like some _____?
   Yes, please!

2 Read and circle the incorrect word. Then write the correct word and say with a partner.

1. Can I have chicken and rice, please?
   Sure. Here you go.
   Thank you.
   _____

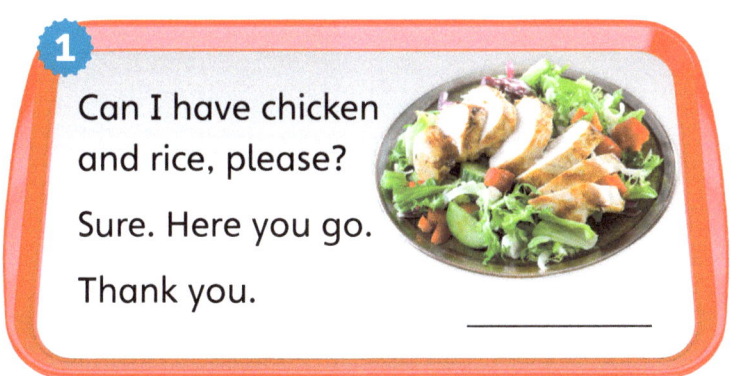

2. Can I have some bread, soup, and water, please?
   Yes. Here you go.
   Thanks.
   _____

Values Be kind. Ask people what they like and don't like.

3 Work with a partner. Ask, answer, and draw.

Would you like chicken today?

No, thank you. Can I have some pasta, please!

Sure!

4 Do you know what food your friends like and don't like? Say.

seventy-five 75

PROJECT AND REVIEW

Create a class meal

Step 1

Research

> What foods do I need?

- [ ] Write a food survey.
- [ ] Ask and answer.
- [ ] Record the answers.

Do you like:

- chicken? [ ]
- rice? [ ]
- salad? [ ]

Step 2

Plan

> What foods do my friends like?

- [ ] Look at your results.
- [ ] Choose foods that a lot of people like.
- [ ] What foods are good together?
- [ ] Plan a meal.

Bar chart:
- chicken: 15
- rice: 25
- salad: 20
- ice cream: 30

Step 3

Create

> How can I make my meal?

- [ ] Look at your plan.
- [ ] Draw or stick the food on paper plates.
- [ ] Design and make a menu.

Pasta, chicken, and cheese
Ice cream and mango
Grapes and watermelon

Have a picnic with your friends.

I like bread and cheese and apples!

Me, too!

Step 4

Show and tell

> Role-play a restaurant scene.

Student A
Ask for your favorite food.

Student B
You are a waiter. Do you have that food?

Can I have some pasta, chicken, and cheese?

Sure! Here you go!

Now I can ...

... use food words.

... ask for things politely using **Can I have ...?**

... ask and answer about objects using **this / that**.

... ask and answer about food.

seventy-seven 77

6 Sports Day

How can I organize a sports day?

1 What sports do you like? Point and say.

2 Stick the items on the picture.

78 seventy-eight

3 Order the pictures. Write 1–4.

CODE CRACKER

a b c d

4 Listen and point. Then sing along and dance.

SONG TIME

Hooray for Sports Day!

Hooray! Hooray!
It's Sports Day today!
Are you **running**? Are you **throwing**?
Are you **jumping** very high?
Yes, I'm running and I'm jumping!
Let's get the balls and throw them in the sky!
I can run, I can jump,
I can swim and I can climb!
Hooray! Hooray! It's Sports Day today,
And I'm having a wonderful time! *x2*

run

jump!

throw

Do you play soccer?
VOCABULARY

I will learn sport and activity words.

1 Listen, point, and repeat.

1. table tennis
2. volleyball 
3. soccer 
4. basketball 
5. team 
6. kick 
7. throw 
8. catch 
9. watch 
10. hit 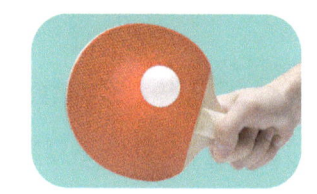
11. jump 
12. run 

2 Match and write.

1. _____ 
2. _____ 
3. _____ 
4. _____

a    b    c 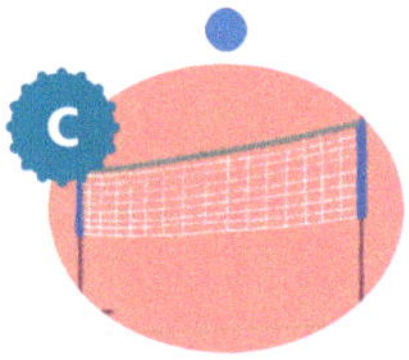   d

3 Ask and answer with a partner.

Do you play volleyball?

Yes! And basketball. What about you?

80 eighty

4 Look at pictures 1–7 and write. Use words from 1. Then write the words for each sport.

basketball	volleyball	table tennis	soccer

5 Work with a partner. Ask and answer.

Do you run in soccer?

Yes, you do!

Do you kick in table tennis?

No, you don't!

6 Make your own picture dictionary. Add your favorite sport words.

kick

table tennis

eighty-one 81

Language lab 1

GRAMMAR 1: I'M JUMPING

I will talk about actions using **I'm ...ing**.

I'm jumping
= I am jumping.

You're jumping
= You are jumping.

Are you swimming?
No, I'm not.

Are you jumping?
Yes, I am.

1 Watch. Then write *Anna* or *Leo*.

1 I'm throwing. _____

2 I'm watching. _____

2 Who is it? Look, match, and write 1–6.

reading   swimming   climbing   kicking   running   throwing

a I'm kicking a ball. ____

b I'm swimming. ____

c I'm running. ____

d I'm throwing. ____

e I'm reading. ____

f I'm climbing. ____

82 eighty-two

3 Listen and check ✓ a, b, or c.

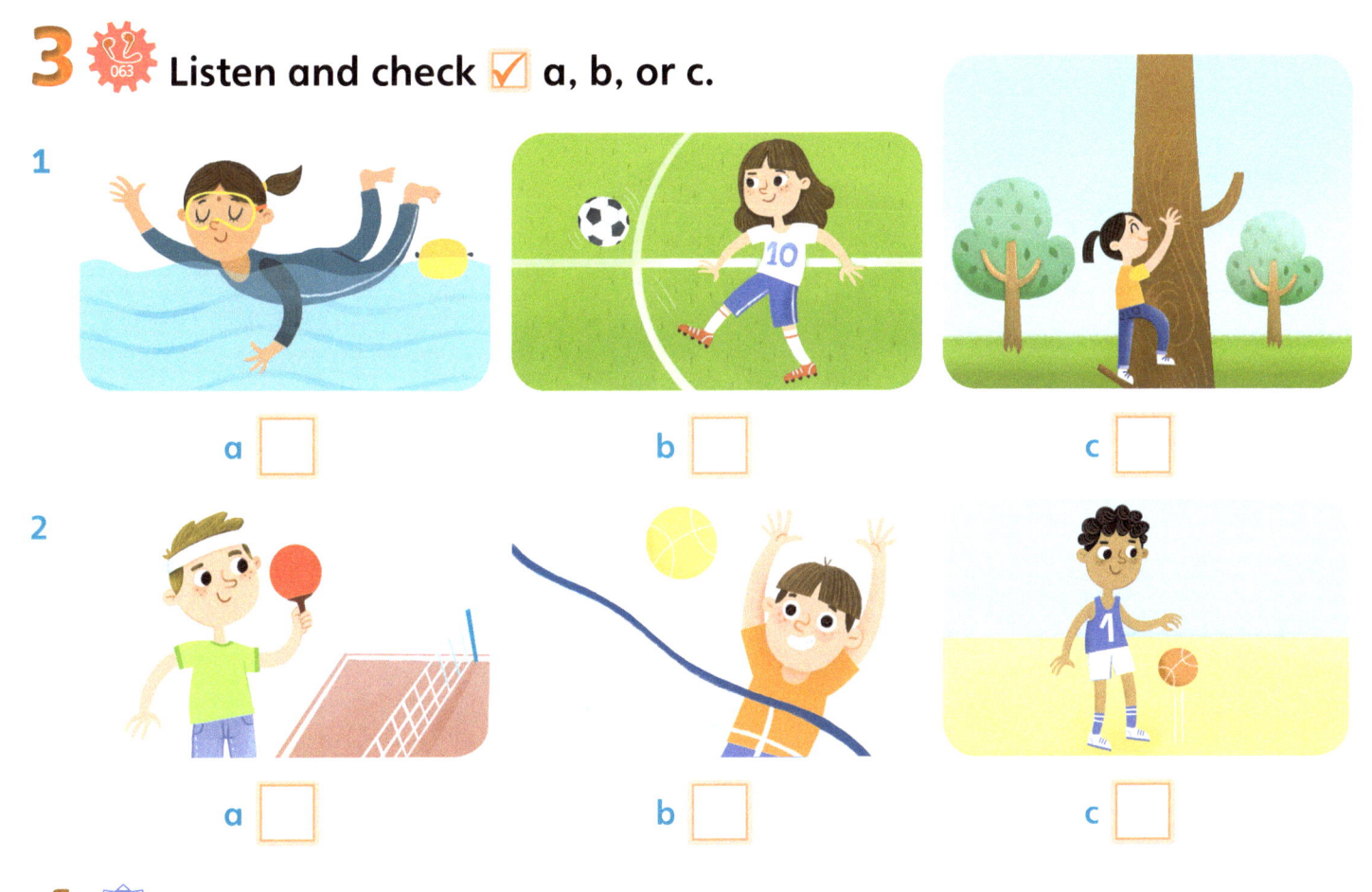

1
- a ☐
- b ☐
- c ☐

2
- a ☐
- b ☐
- c ☐

4 Write. Then check ✓ the activities you like. Act them out. Say I'm …

1 I'm _____   2 _____   3 _____   4 _____

5 Make a sports person. Then play a guessing game.

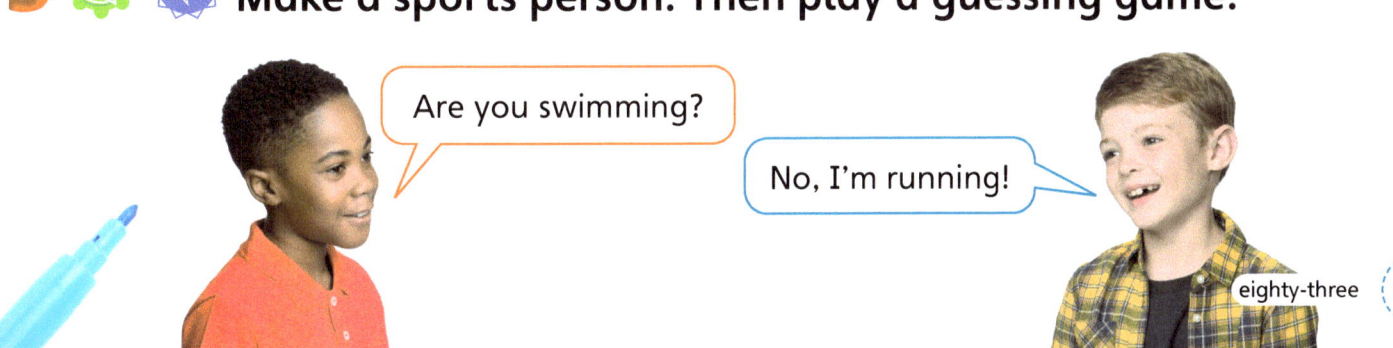

Are you swimming?

No, I'm running!

eighty-three 83

Story lab
READING

I will read a story about a game of soccer.

1 🎧 💬 **Read and listen. What are the two teams called?**

GOAL!

1 Good luck, Castle School!
Look at Milly! She likes soccer!

2 Run, Anna! Are you running, Leo?
I'm running!
I'm not running. I'm jumping!

3 Goal!
Great goal, Leo!

4 Goal!
The score is River School 1, Castle School 1.

2 💡 **Who says it? Choose and write.**

Miss Kelly   Tom   Leo   Anna

1 I'm running! _____   2 I'm not running! _____
3 I'm jumping! _____   4 I'm kicking! _____
5 I'm coming! _____   6 You're playing soccer! _____

84 eighty-four

5 Kick, Leo! / I'm kicking!

6 Ow! My leg! / I'm coming, Leo!

7 Goal! / Great goal, Milly! You're playing soccer!

8 River School 1, Castle School 1, and Milly 1!

3 Read. How many goals in total?

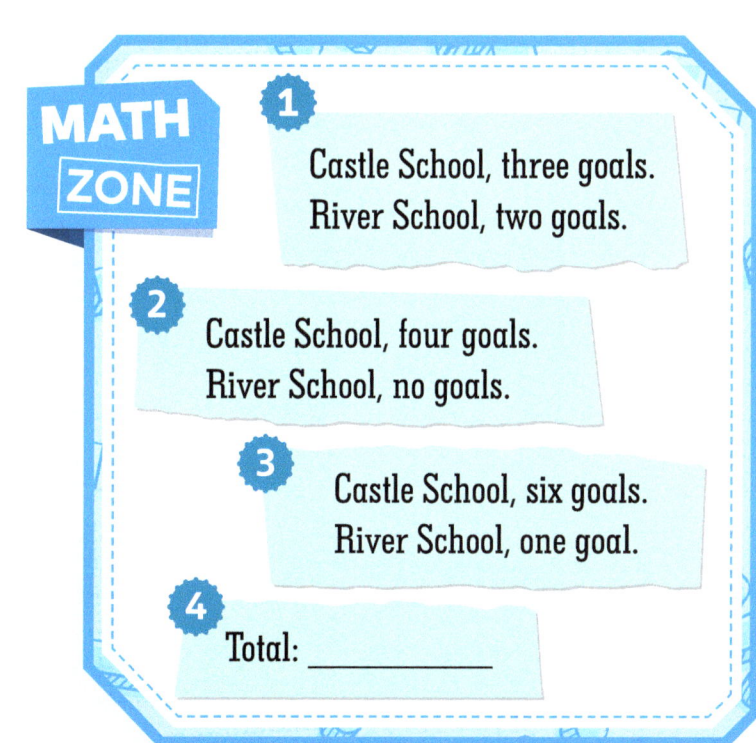

MATH ZONE

1. Castle School, three goals. River School, two goals.

2. Castle School, four goals. River School, no goals.

3. Castle School, six goals. River School, one goal.

4. Total: _____

4 Circle. Then listen and check.

River school are **1** yellow / red , and Castle School are **2** green / blue !

Yes! Goal!

Castle School **3** 1 / 2 , River School 0!

Oh, now a goal for River School!

4 River / My School 1, Castle School 1.

5 Act out the story in groups.

Phonics lab
TH

I will learn the th sounds.

1 **Listen and repeat. Then write th.**

1 ___at    2 ___ese    3 ___ere    4 ___ank    5 ___irteen    6 ___row

2 **Listen and chant.**

They have this and that, this and that.
They have these and those, these and those!

Throw three things!
Throw three things!
Three things, three things,
Throw three things!

3 **Listen and play the game.**

this, that, these, those

thank, three, thirteen, throw

4 **Read. Write the next th word.**

CODE CRACKER

1	this	that	this	that
	_____			
2	three	thirteen	thirteen	three
	_____			
3	thank	thing	throw	thank
	_____			

Experiment lab

MATH: MEASURING

I will learn about measuring things in sports.

EXPERIMENT TIME

▶ Watch a video about measuring.

1 🎧 **Listen and read.**

lungs

In many sports, we measure things. We measure how far we can jump or run or swim. We measure how high we can jump. We measure how high a table tennis net is. We measure how big a soccer field is. We measure how big a basketball court is.

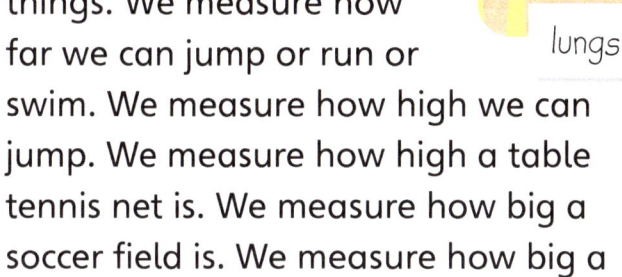

We can measure the air in our lungs, too!

2 Look and circle.

I'm jumping / measuring.
How far you can jump? Say.

3 💡 Read and write the answer.

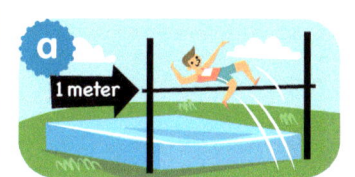

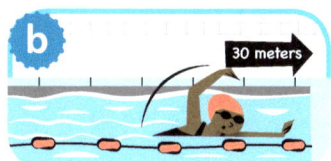

a — 1 meter
b — 30 meters

1 How far can she swim?

   She can swim _____ meters.

2 How high can he jump?

   He can jump _____ meter.

How much air is in your lungs? How far can you blow?

1 Blow and measure.

One blow!

How big is your balloon?

_____ centimeters?

2 Circle for you.

There is a lot of / a little air in my lungs.

3 Find and measure the objects. Then complete the chart.

	How many centimeters?
✏️	
🥢	

eighty-seven 87

Language lab 2

GRAMMAR 2: CAN YOU ...?

*I will ask and answer about actions using **Can you ...?***

1 Choose and write. Then check ✓ the correct answer.

swim   Can   you

Can you ride a bike?
Yes, **I can**.   No, **I can't**.

1 Can you _____ ?   Yes, I can. ☐   No, I can't. ☐
2 _____ you climb this wall?   Yes, I can. ☐   No, I can't. ☐
3 Can _____ kick?   Yes, I can. ☐   No, I can't. ☐

2 Can you do it? Try. Then write Yes, I can or No, I can't.

1. Can you draw an octopus?
_____

2. Can you dance and say: "A fox in a box."?
_____

3. Can you throw and catch two balls?
_____

4. Can you jump and sing?
_____

3 Make a throwing game. Then play with a partner.

Can you do this?
No. Can you?
Yes!
Well done!

Can you juggle?
COMMUNICATION

I will talk about activities with my friends.

1 🎧 070 **Listen and read. Circle the correct word.**

1. Can you juggle? — What does juggle / jump mean?
2. You throw and catch / kick two balls. Can you juggling / juggle? — Yes / No, I can't!
3. I can help you! Watch me! Are you juggle / juggling? — Yes, I am! I'm juggling! Thank you!

2 💬 **Learn to juggle. Then say.**

JUGGLE WITH TWO HATS!

I'm throwing!

Now I'm catching!

Now juggle with balls!

Values I share my skills and help my friends to do things.

3 💬 **Ask and answer with a partner. Write yes or no.**

Can you do this?

	Me	My partner	We can help each other.
Yoga!			
Hula hoop!			

4 💬 **What new skills can you teach a friend? Say.**

PROJECT AND REVIEW

Organize a Sports Day

Step 1

Research

▷ What will our Sports Day include?

☐ Ask classmates what games and sports they can play.

☐ Choose our favorites.

	Table tennis	Hula hoop	Balloon volleyball
Sofia	✓	✓	✓
Darios	✓	✗	✓
Chen	✗	✓	✓

Can you play balloon volleyball?

No!

I can help you.

Thanks!

Step 2

Plan

▷ What do we need to do?

☐ Choose a place to do the activities.

☐ Make a list of things we need.

☐ Decide what we need to make.

We have	We don't have
balls	balloons

90 ninety

Step 3

Create

> How can we organize our Sports Day?

- [ ] Prepare the space for your day.
- [ ] Create your games.
- [ ] Draw and write a program.

Our Sports Day
- Balloon volleyball
- Sack race
- Table tennis

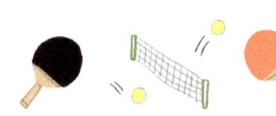

Watch your friends play sports and cheer them on.

Great game!

Step 4

Show and tell

> Play the games and sports.

- [ ] Help each other.

I'm in the sack race.

Are you running in the sack?

No. You can't run in a sack. I'm jumping.

Now I can ...

- ... use sport and activity words.
- ... talk about actions using **I'm ...ing**.
- ... ask and answer about actions using **Can you ...?**
- ... talk about activities with my friends.

ninety-one 91

Amazing boat races

CULTURE 3

1 Look at the pictures. What do you think they are doing?

2 Listen and read.

I'm watching boats on a river. It's a boat race!

Zongzi is my favorite food!

Dragon boats

It is the Dragon Boat Festival in Yueyang, in China. The Dragon Boat festival is in June.

There are lots of teams in boats. The boats are beautiful colors. There are dragon heads on the boats.

You sit down in the dragon boats. There are drums on the boats, too. This man is hitting a drum.

There is special food for the festival. Zongzi is made with rice. There are leaves around the rice.

Gondolas

These boats are called gondolas. They are in Venice, in Italy. Every year, in September, there is a gondola race. The boats are very beautiful. They are red and yellow and silver and gold. You stand up in the gondolas.

This famous food from Venice is called rise e bise in Italian. It's delicious!

Fun Fact!
The winners of the gondola race get red flags!

92 ninety-two

3 Read and circle the correct answer.

1. The Dragon Boat race is in Italy / China .
2. The gondola race is in Italy / China .
3. There is a drum on the Dragon Boats / gondolas .
4. You stand up in Dragon Boats / gondolas .
5. They win flags in the Dragon Boat race / Gondola race .
6. Zongzi is made with rice and leaves / rice and peas .

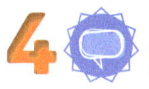

4 Imagine you are at the boat races. Ask and answer.

> I'm watching dragon boats.

> You're in China!

My Culture

Find out about traditional or famous boat races in your country.

5 Make a Dragon Boat.

1. Cut out some card.
2. Draw some lines.
3. Fold the card.
4. Use sticky tape.
5. Stick the coins.
6. Make a dragon head and tail. Your boat is ready!

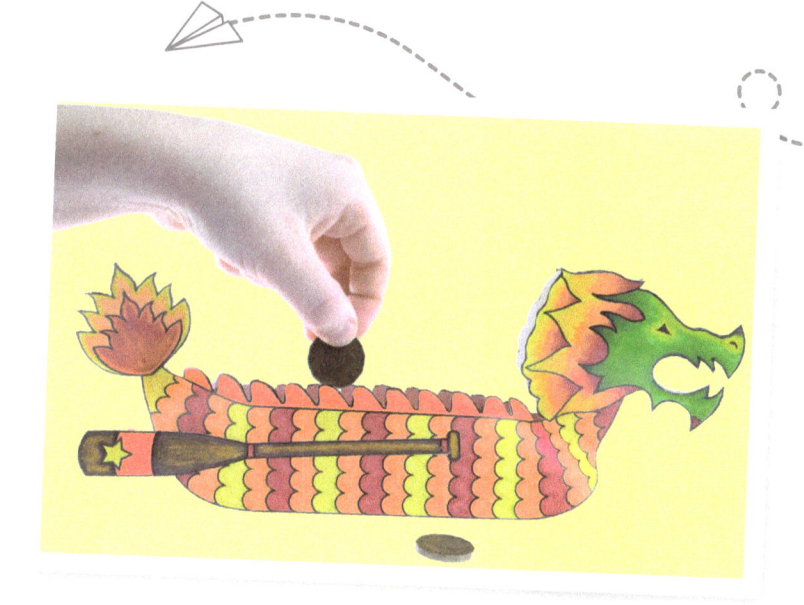

> This is my Dragon Boat. This is the dragon head!

6 Describe your boat to your partner.

Wordlist

Unit 1

Directions Vocabulary
down
left
right
straight
up

Natural World Vocabulary
bridge
cloud
flower
forest
hill
path
tree

Phonics lab
cheese
cherry
chicken
jeep
juice
jump
see
shell
shoe
shop
soup
sun

Experiment lab
hills
land
landforms
layers
mountains
push
rocks
tectonic plates
towels
volcanoes

Unit 2

Places Vocabulary
café
castle
farm
house
library
museum
park
playground
river
school
store
swimming pool

Phonics lab
bag
cap
cat
leg
man
mat
pan
clap
pen
peg
pet
ten
wet

Experiment lab
bricks
cement
spaghetti
steel
straws
strong
tower
wood

Culture 1

beautiful
Cornwall
England
fresh
garden
giants
grass
oxygen
roof
secret
Singapore
walls

Unit 3

Animals Vocabulary

bat
cow
donkey
goat
owl
porcupine

Daily Routine Vocabulary

brush my teeth
eat
go to school
sleep
wake up
wash my face

Phonics lab

dog
fox
hop
hot
jog
frog
stop
bin
hit
sing
sit
win
six

Experiment lab

day
earth
hours
months
night
shines
sky
sun
year

Unit 4

Adjectives for People and Feelings Vocabulary

angry
friendly
funny
happy
helpful
kind
lazy
naughty
sad
shy
tired
young

Phonics lab

jacket
jaguar
jar
jeans
jog
juice
jump
jungle
yak
yellow
yes
yo-yo

ninety-five 95

Wordlist

yogurt
you
young
yours

Experiment lab

eyebrows
eyes
face
muscles
mouths
noses
artist
yawn

Culture 2

bagpipes
blow
drums
flute
India
instrument
Japan
neck
pipes
Scotland
sticks
strings
traditional
veena

Unit 5

Food and Drink Vocabulary

bread
cheese
chicken
cookies
fish
ice cream
juice
pasta
rice
salad
soup
water

Phonics lab

chair
cheese
cherries
chess
chicken
chips
sheep
shelf
ship
shirt
shoes
shop
shorts

Experiment lab

almonds
coconuts
farmer
combine harvester
factory
ice cream
milk
nuts
pick
plants
soybeans
vanilla
healthy
machine

Unit 6

Sports Vocabulary

basketball
catch
hit
jump
kick
run
soccer
table tennis
team
throw
volleyball
watch

Phonics lab
thank
that
there
these
they
thing
thirteen
this
those
three
throw

Experiment lab
air
blow
court
far
field
important
centimeters
lungs
match
measure
measuring
meter
net

Culture 3
China
dragon
flag
festival
gold cup
gondola
hitting
Italy
leaves
race
regatta
rice
tail
teams
Venice
winner
Yueyang
Zongzi

Continents
Africa
Antarctica
Asia
Australia
Europe
North America
South America

Grammar Reference

Unit 1

Grammar 1

Imperatives:

Go straight.

Don't go straight.

Turn left.

Don't turn right.

Grammar 2

Preposition of place:

The ball is *under* the table.
The doll is *next to* the box.
The eraser is *on* the shelf.
The car is *in front of* the ball.
The teddy bear is *in* the box.
The hat is *behind* the box.
The book is *near* the eraser.
The ball is *opposite* the doll.
The train is *above* the eraser.

Unit 2

Grammar 1

Present Simple with *like* (affirmative, negative, and question form):

I *like* cats. I *don't like* frogs.
He *likes* dogs.
She *doesn't like* birds.

Does Tom *like* horses?
Yes, he does./
No, he doesn't.

Grammar 2

There's/There are ...

There*'s* a mouse.   There *are* frogs.
There *isn't* a rabbit.   There *aren't* any fish.

98　ninety-eight

Unit 3

Grammar 1

Present Simple for routines and general truths (affirmative, negative, and question form):

I go to the park. *I don't go* to school.
We play soccer. *We don't play* music.
You eat in the café. *You don't eat* in the car.
They go to the store. *They don't go* to the farm.

On Saturdays, *do you go* to school? No, I don't.

Do you play soccer? Yes, I do.

Grammar 2

Present Simple for routines and general truths (affirmative, negative, and question form):

She eats a banana every day.
He doesn't ride his bike every day.

Does he swim every day?
Yes, *he does*. No, *he doesn't*.

Grammar Reference

Unit 4

Grammar 1

be verb (third person affirmative, negative, and question form):

Is he angry?
No, he *isn't*. He*'s* tired.

Is she shy?
Yes, she *is*.

Is she sad?
No, she *isn't*.

Adverbs of frequency: always/sometimes/never

She *is always* shy.
He *is sometimes* tired.
She *is never* naughty.

Grammar 2

Have for possession (question form):

Do you have a lizard?
Yes, *I do*.

Do you have a goat?
No, *I don't*.

It's and *its*

It's my lizard! *It's* friendly. *Its* tail is green.
Its eyes are orange. *It's* never angry.

100 one hundred

Unit 5

Grammar 1

Can for permission (question form and natural answers):

Can I have some building blocks, please?
Sure!

Can I have a pear, please?
Sorry, no!

Grammar 2

Can for permission (question form with this/that for proximity):

Can I have *this* book, please?
This one?
Yes!

Can I have *that* ball, please?
That one?
Yes!

Can I have a teddy bear, please?
This one or *that* one?
This one!

Unit 6

Grammar 1

Present Progressive (first person affirmative statements, questions, and short form answers):

I'm eating.

You're sleeping.

Are you drinking water?
Yes, *I am*.

Are you running?
No, *I'm not*.

Grammar 2

Can for ability (question form)

Can you fly?
Yes, I *can*.

Can you climb trees?
No, I *can't*.

one hundred and one 101

Irregular verbs

	Present Simple	Past Simple
be	I am You are He/She/It is We are They are	I was You were He/She/It was We were They were
be able to	I can You can He/She/It can We can They can	I could You could He/She/It could We could They could
draw	I draw You draw He/She/It draws We draw They draw	I drew You drew He/She/It drew We drew They drew
drink	I drink You drink He/She/It drinks We drink They drink	I drank You drank He/She/It drank We drank They drank
eat	I eat You eat He/She/It eats We eat They eat	I ate You ate He/She/It ate We ate They ate
go	I go You go He/She/It goes We go They go	I went You went He/She/It went We went They went
have	I have You have He/She/It has We have They have	I had You had He/She/It had We had They had

	Present Simple	Past Simple
make	I make You make He/She/It makes We make They make	I made You made He/She/It made We made They made
run	I run You run He/She/It runs We run They run	I ran You ran He/She/It ran We ran They ran
sing	I sing You sing He/She/It sings We sing They sing	I sang You sang He/She/It sang We sang They sang
sleep	I sleep You sleep He/She/It sleeps We sleep They sleep	I slept You slept He/She/It slept We slept They slept
swim	I swim You swim He/She/It swims We swim They swim	I swam You swam He/She/It swam We swam They swam
throw	I throw You throw He/She/It throws We throw They throw	I threw You threw He/She/It threw We threw They threw
wake	I wake You wake He/She/It wakes We wake They wake	I woke You woke He/She/It woke We woke They woke

OUR WORLD

INTRO:
Here we stand: children of every age,
This is our world and the world's our stage.
We can laugh, we can cry — we can float, we can fly,
We can dance, we can sing — we can do almost anything
in OUR world ... our *beautiful* world.

VERSE 1:
Some of us are small; some of us are tall,
Some of us are shy; some of us say hi to everybody,
Some of us like numbers; some of us love words,
Some of us watch football, and some of us watch the birds!

(CHORUS)
This is *our* world ... we're different but the same.
We live and learn together — we get to know each other ...
in OUR world ... our *beautiful* world.

VERSE 2:
Some of us like music; some of us like cars,
Some of us see pictures, looking at the stars,
Some of us are scientists, trying to find the code,
All of us can help a friend and give a hand to hold.

This is *our* world — there's room for everyone.
We learn to live together, and we have a lot of fun ...
In *our* world ... in ***our*** world ... in our beautiful world!

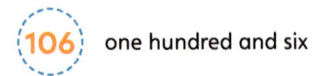

English Code

Journey

Level 2

CERTIFICATE

WELL DONE!

_____

Student's Name

_____

Teacher's Signature and Date

Pearson

1 Our world
PHONICS LAB: *S*, *SH*, *J* AND *CH*

4 Make shell shapes.

Press-out

5 Come in!
PHONICS LAB: *CH* AND *SH*

Press-out

4 **Make shapes and play with a partner.**

Amazing boat races
CULTURE: ORIGAMI BOAT PART 1

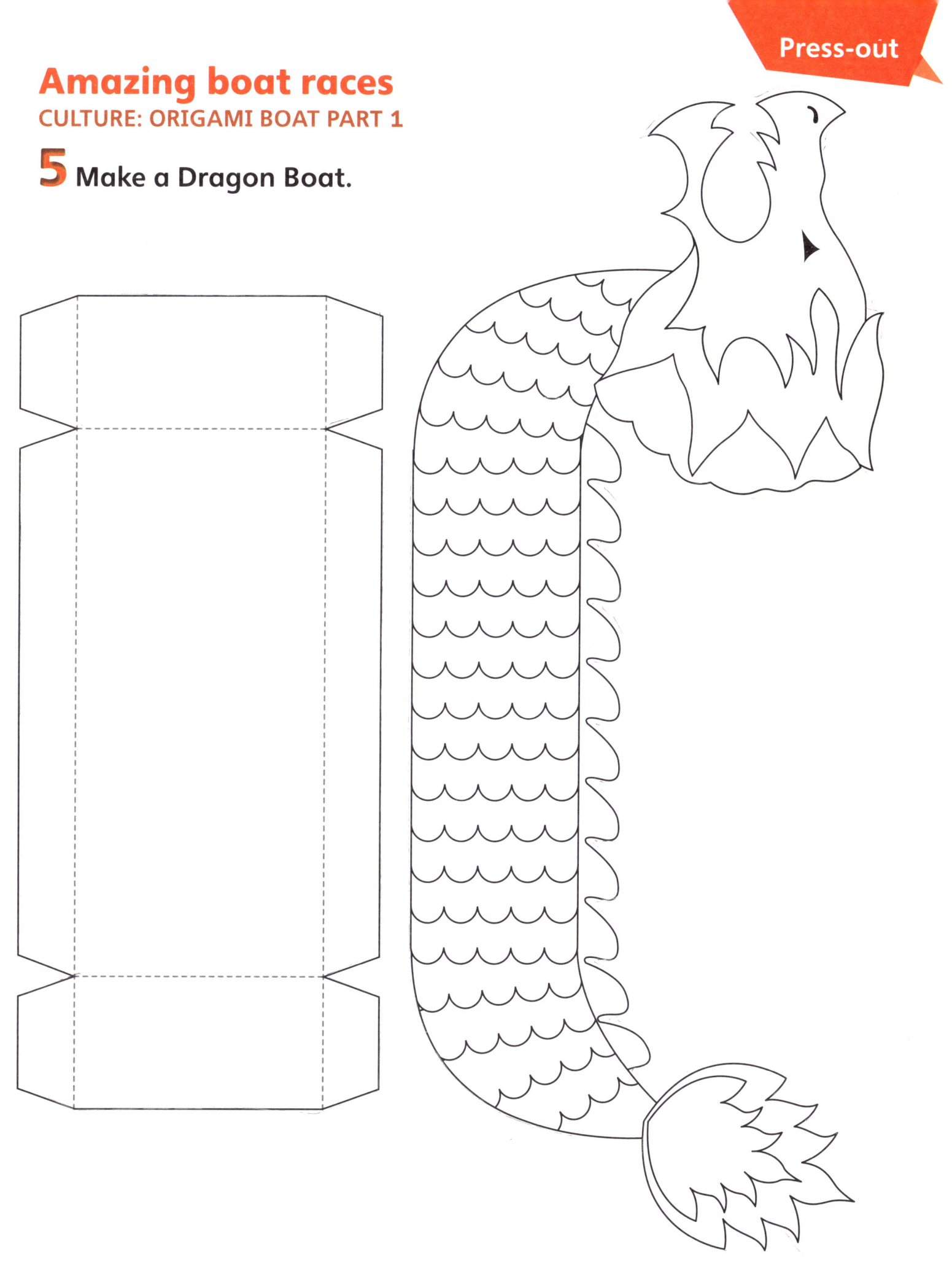

5 Make a Dragon Boat.

Press-out

Amazing boat races
CULTURE: ORIGAMI BOAT PART 2

Press-out

Stickers

1. Our world

pages 4–5

2. Out and about!

pages 18–19

3. Day and night

pages 34–35

4. At the gallery

Stickers

pages 48–49

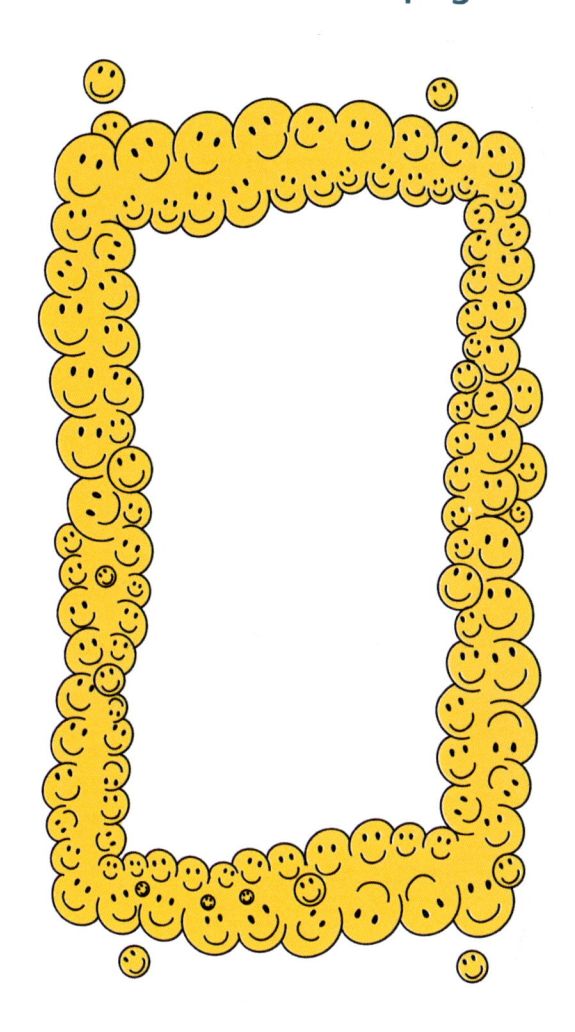

5. Come in!

pages 64–65

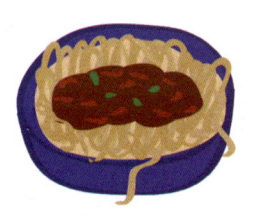

6. Sports Day

Stickers

pages 78–79

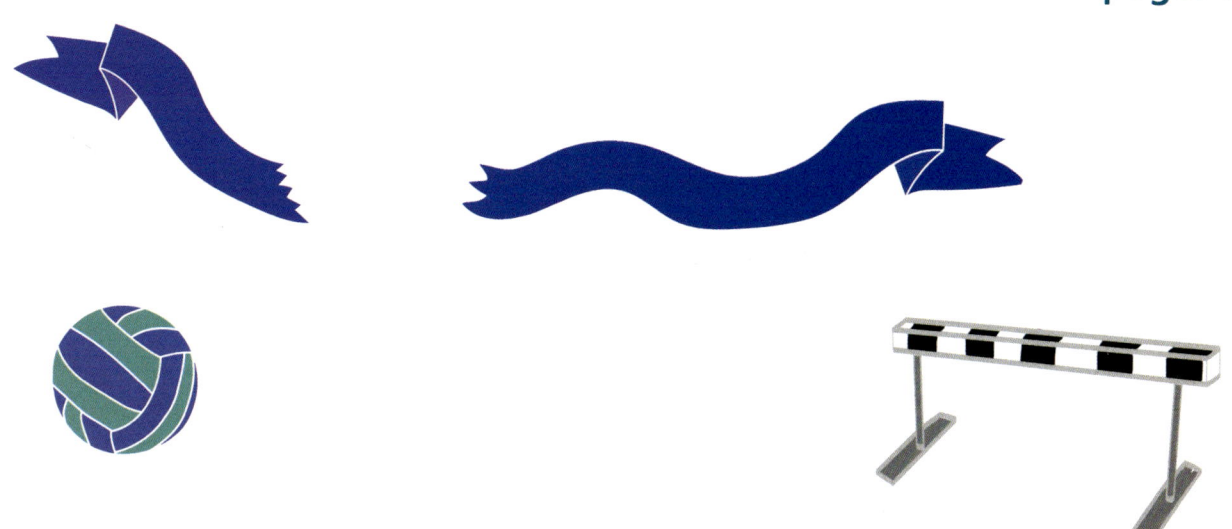

Now I can ...

Stickers